T0328694

Cambridge Elements ≡

Elements in Travel Writing
edited by
Nandini Das
University of Oxford
Tim Youngs
Nottingham Trent University

WRITING MOBILE LIVES, 1500–1700

Eva Johanna Holmberg
University of Helsinki

CAMBRIDGE
UNIVERSITY PRESS

Shaftesbury Road, Cambridge CB2 8EA, United Kingdom

One Liberty Plaza, 20th Floor, New York, NY 10006, USA

477 Williamstown Road, Port Melbourne, VIC 3207, Australia

314–321, 3rd Floor, Plot 3, Splendor Forum, Jasola District Centre,
New Delhi – 110025, India

103 Penang Road, #05–06/07, Visioncrest Commercial, Singapore 238467

Cambridge University Press is part of Cambridge University Press & Assessment,
a department of the University of Cambridge.

We share the University's mission to contribute to society through the pursuit of
education, learning and research at the highest international levels of excellence.

www.cambridge.org
Information on this title: www.cambridge.org/9781009507431

DOI: 10.1017/9781009180726

First published 2024

A catalogue record for this publication is available from the British Library.

ISBN 978-1-009-50743-1 Hardback
ISBN 978-1-009-18073-3 Paperback
ISSN 2632-7090 (online)
ISSN 2632-7082 (print)

Cambridge University Press & Assessment has no responsibility for the persistence
or accuracy of URLs for external or third-party internet websites referred to in this
publication and does not guarantee that any content on such websites is, or will
remain, accurate or appropriate.

Writing Mobile Lives, 1500–1700

Elements in Travel Writing

DOI: 10.1017/9781009180726
First published online: March 2024

Eva Johanna Holmberg
University of Helsinki

Author for correspondence: Eva Johanna Holmberg, eva.holmberg@helsinki.fi

Abstract: This Element develops and showcases a new methodological framework in which to study the connections between early modern travel writing and life- and self-writing. Turning the scholarly focus in the study of travel writing from eyewitnessing and proto-ethnography of foreign lands to the 'fashioned' and portrayed selves and 'inner worlds' of travellers – personal memory, autobiographical practices, and lived yet often heavily mediated travel experiences – it opens up perspectives to travel writing in its many modes, that extend both before and after 'lived' travels into their many pre- and afterlives in textual form. This title is also available as Open Access on Cambridge Core.

Keywords: mobility, autobiography, early modern travel writing, cultural history, travel

ISBNs: 9781009507431 (HB), 9781009180733 (PB), 9781009180726 (OC)
ISSNs: 2632-7090 (online), 2632-7082 (print)

Contents

1 Introduction

This Element explores early modern English manuscripts and printed travel accounts as efforts to record travellers' mobile lives, turning our gaze to the 'inner worlds' and lives of travellers. It approaches travellers' writings both as records and expressions of their experiences and as avenues for their descriptions and 'fashionings' of the self, investigating the many ways travellers' texts were both drinking from the autobiographical font and contributing to it. In doing this, the Element recalibrates scholarship on early modern travel and travel writing and offers a change in perspective: rather than exploring a traveller's gaze towards the foreign, or continuing on the tried and tested paths of studying early modern travel – from pilgrimage to Grand Tour – as a separate and somewhat decontextualised, even esoteric topic, it considers travel writing as a form of life writing, simultaneously turning the gaze both inwards and outwards. It suggests we explore how travellers described their journeys while also writing themselves and their inner lives and embodied experiences into the story. This move, I argue, provides not only new rich evidence about travel in this period but also helps to show how and why mobility mattered deeply to early modern people and should thus be brought back to the mainstream of scholarly discussions of this period (Williams 2019; Gallagher 2017). Paying more attention to travel writing as a form of life writing will also help us read travel and travellers' experiences in a more nuanced way, equipped with decades of new work on mobility, life writing, and histories of embodied experience (Holmberg 2017).

Travel writing has often been dismissed from the fold of 'ego documents' or life writing on the grounds that its focus is not, or at least not sufficiently, on the description of lives and 'the self' of its authors (Summerfield 2019, pp. 4–5).[1] However, rather than drawing boundaries between what might have constituted 'travel writing' and 'life writing' in this period – a useless task, as people did not have a clear idea of such generic boundaries in this period – this Element aims to explore their meeting points and entanglements with the help of three case studies. Early modern genres were fuzzy and constantly overlapping, even when they were interpreted or imposed by later researchers, and there is no real consensus over the meaning of 'life writing', 'ego document', or autobiographical text in this period (Hadfield 2009; Legassie 2017; Rubiés 2000a; Stewart 2018). Therefore, in our future studies, it seems essential to explore the shared overlaps, borrowings, citationality, and varied forms of travel and life writings, rather than search for any clear categories. Focusing our efforts only on the printed single-authored accounts of travel prioritises a certain type of

---

[1] Historians, especially in the German speaking academia and the Netherlands, have been fonder of the term 'ego-documents' rather than other concepts describing the writing of the self.

traveller (i.e. white, elite, and male, admittedly the types of traveller even this study concentrates on) over others and allows other types (i.e. mobile non-elites, women, and people of colour) to fall through the cracks altogether. Moreover, this kind of fuzziness, or even 'messiness' with boundaries, allows early modern mobility to appear as a richer and messier phenomenon, while at the same time interrogating travel accounts with as much nuance as any early modern autobiographical account and reveals them as fascinating sources for histories of experience (Holmberg 2019).

Due to and enabled by the aforementioned slippery early modern genre-boundaries, travel themes often cropped up in and were 'travelling' between texts that have not previously been investigated as vehicles or receptacles of travel writing. These textual forms included manuscripts, commonplace books, family books, logbooks, diaries, spiritual autobiographies, and miscellaneous notebooks. Some of the texts processed and recorded themes that were eventually published, while some remained in manuscripts (Wyatt 2021). These texts offer both new data and material insights into the preservation and recording of travel experiences, and how travellers selected, processed, and decided what to preserve about themselves and their travels for posterity. Investigating a wider variety of texts as not only travel writing but also as life writing allows for the inclusion and investigation of a greater variety of travellers from diverse social backgrounds. In addition, this type of investigation helps us to see how writing and recording itself could 'travel' between genres and textual forms into more polished accounts in manuscripts and published travel collections and compilations. Such investigations will also allow the discovery of avenues for life writing and self-recording outside the later 'dominant templates' of the diary and the autobiography, as shown by Adam Smyth among others (Amelang 1998; Smyth 2010). Sources of manuscript travel accounts include textual forms such as almanacs and financial account books and can be approached as rich presentations of the self that were often in motion, similar to their mobile authors.[2] Investigating these texts requires interdisciplinarity and a broad set of methodological tools that have been developed to capture the richness of human experience, ranging from autobiography, life writing, and material texts to the study of the history of lived and embodied experience, including the history of emotions and senses. All of these will be tackled more fully in the sections that follow (Canning 1994; Boddice 2023).

---

[2] Smyth and Laura Ambrose have shown how shorter journeys were recorded in almanacs (Ambrose 2013). Financial accounting can be detected in manuscript travel accounts when travellers kept records of the course, duration and cost of their journeys, often noting them in meticulous detail, although they can be detected even in printed accounts aimed at larger audiences ranging from Fynes Moryson's *Itinerary* to Thomas Coryate's *Crudities*, among others.

Where can we look for the travellers' 'self', their subjectivity, or even a small part of their often-elusive experiences as travellers? At first glance, it might seem that pilgrimage modes and narratives granted more room to explore the inner spiritual life and pursuits of a pilgrim, whereas secular travel by traders, diplomats, and educational travellers such as the 'Grand Tourists' would have focused more on the production of knowledge of foreign lands. However, this kind of division is unhelpful when we want to appreciate the richness of early modern travellers' experiences and the many contexts and modes of their writing (Holmberg 2019). In fact, travellers' descriptions of their embodied experiences and secular interests cropped up in pilgrimage reports and secular accounts alike, in the descriptions of illness and ailing, efforts to visualise their experiences and persona, and practices of still commemorating and writing about their travels a long time after the travels had ended. In addition to the more ephemeral sources of travel experience, like the often-vanishing materiality and objects related to travels, it is vital we reconsider traditional sources such as logbooks, letters, and travel diaries and also other well-trodden tracks of retrospective travel writing from new angles. As is typical of writers in general, historians tend to gravitate towards individuals and stories that resonate with them; thus, we need to remember that our stories should reflect the diversity of the early modern world. This research practice throws light on the overlap and shared ways of thinking of aristocratic and elite travellers, travellers from the merchant class, and people who tended to fall in between or outside these categories such as women, servants, mariners, or marginalised people.

This introduction aims to take stock of the range of possible approaches to writing about travellers' mobile lives in auto/biographical, historical, and literary studies – not a small task. It will also suggest and present some new ways to write cultural histories of mobile people, engaging with scholarly approaches such as global microhistories, history of experiences, emotions, and senses; and, perhaps more critically, with the immediate theoretical backgrounds in the study of Renaissance individualism, 'self-fashioning', and literary identity formation. All these approaches and some of their tools (if honed and focused onto mobile people) could and should be employed in the study of both more 'genre-conforming' travel writing and other miscellaneous texts that were the products of early modern mobility. When we focus our gaze on the central figure of the traveller, equipped with these tools, we gain more insight not only into the process of the production of these varied texts but also their social motivations and ideological aims, without reverting to the old ways of simplistic and anachronistic psychological explanation of the intentions of traveller 'authors' and their individual sensibilities. My wider claim is that we are missing the lens through which early modern people themselves saw and described their world;

that is, we fundamentally misunderstand these texts unless we look at them through the lens of autobiography and life writing. This Element develops this discussion by making three essential claims and contributions:

1. Embodiment is one of the most direct routes to the self in travel writing.
2. Considering a wider range of travel writing types will acknowledge a greater range of people than the traditional historiography of travel.
3. In our reading, we need to appreciate how most travel writing is retrospective and commemorative, not just of individual travellers but also of their experiences and social relations.

The field of Renaissance studies has a complex history of discussions about individuality and the self as a result of the foundational stones laid by Burckhardt and a vibrant and ongoing interest in autobiographical and biographical studies (Martin 2018; Dragstra, Ottway, and Wilcox 2000). The range of studies has expanded from those of 'great' men and women to include studies of 'exceptional typical' individuals in microhistories, group biographies, and studies of local communities that explore the contours of their agency/ies (Farr and Ruggiero 2019). Scholarly discussions have likewise moved on from debates about the various 'births' of individuality during the European Renaissance to investigating the framings, representations, fashioning, and boundary-making regarding the 'self'; Greenblatt's *Renaissance Self-Fashioning* inspired the most discussion about the limits of performance and individual agency in literary representations of the self (Coleman, Lewis, and Kowalik 2000; Haydon 2017; Mayer and Woolf eds. 1995; Sharpe and Zwicker 2008).[3] The well-worn dictum about 'travellers lying by authority' and the suspicions directed at both autobiographies and travellers might cause us to assume that travel writers' strategic motivations and 'self-fashioning' resulted in both their 'real' lived experiences and lives becoming 'hidden' from view, and that travel developed into a self-reflective practice only later in the eighteenth century (Hadfield 2017). However, the fact that something is 'fashioned' or 'performative' does not mean it is untrue or that a narrative has no basis in lived experience; this study does not aim to discover all the lies and deceptions of travellers (that would be really boring indeed), but rather attempts to trace the wider contours and meanings they gave to their mobility in the context of their lives.

Currently, individual identity is increasingly seen in the context of the manifold relationships between early modern people and their changing settings and communities, shaped, produced, and represented in intersecting social and

---

[3] Historian Peter Burke was inspired by Greenblatt to write *The Fabrication of Louis XIV* (1992), and many others followed suit.

cultural formations, occupational roles, and relations (Hailwood and Waddell 2023; Paul 2018; Shepard 2015; Scott-Warren 2016; Waddell 2019). Scholars have occasionally chosen to emphasise the structures that restricted early modern people, sometimes viewing the contexts they operated in as accommodating them and giving their lives meaning and purpose, often both. Sometimes 'the self' has been approached as more 'relational' and 'social', while other times as a more isolated 'interiority' and entity of an individual experiencing subject (Fullbrook and Rublack 2010). Despite efforts to kill the 'author' or 'agency' in mid-twentieth and twenty-first century literary criticism (along with the change in focus after the linguistic turn to discourse and representation), questions about the shape of the self and the contours of subjectivity did not disappear from the fields of autobiography and life-writing studies, even if separate schools of thought and rifts occasionally appeared between historians and literary scholars who occupied the scholarly territory.[4]

Microhistory, one of the great historical trends after the linguistic turn, has blossomed since Carlo Ginzburg, Natalie Zemon Davis, and others introduced the benefits to history of the combined micro- and macroscopic gaze (N. Davis 1986; N. Davis 1988; L. Davis 2002). Microhistory has provided social and cultural historians an entry to the playing field usually occupied by literary scholars, biographers, and talented storytellers writing for the general public, focusing their historical scholarly gaze not only on famous individuals but also obscure and marginal figures, with the aim of illuminating larger structures and mentalities. The 'global microhistory' approach can supply tools for studying the travelling self, provided it does not succumb to the impulse of only investigating global figures who successfully crossed cultural boundaries and provide inspiration and points of identification for our times and ourselves. In addition to Davis' Leo Africanus, Linda Colley's Elizabeth Marsh or John-Paul Ghobrial's Elias of Babylon, we also need studies of travellers whose 'travails' were perhaps less inspiring, with duller outcomes and scarcer paper trails, from the labouring poor to the servants who travelled in the entourages of princes and aristocrats, or the sailors and mariners who plundered and struggled around the globe (Davis 2006; Colley 2007; Ghobrial 2014). Only by widening our lens in this way will we gain a fuller picture of how people understood their mobility in this period (Ansell 2015; Mansell 2021; Williams 2019). Often the paper trails

---

[4] This has been particularly visible in recent years in the terrain of biography writing and discussions about what constitutes life writing or life writing studies. Historian Hans Renders has been advocating for 'scholarly biographies', whereas Craig Howes considers life writing as a fruitful bridge between disciplinary boundaries (Renders, de Haan, and Harsma 2017). A cultural historian's perspective is often conciliatory, aiming to build interdisciplinary bridges rather than boundaries between disciplines.

go cold, with exceptional or norm-challenging individuals leaving more traces of both themselves and their travels than those less exceptional, but this should not prevent scholars from setting up wider nets to catch their experiences. It has been argued by scholars in mobility studies that we should also try to follow our subjects throughout their whole lives, capturing their 'ongoing' mobilities, returns, and back-and-forth movements, in addition to more direct movements between 'point A and point B'. In this, a more biographical approach truly helps, showing that the same people often travelled beyond the geographical focuses of scholarship on travels in the Levant or South-East Asia. How these practices and experiences of worldwide mobility shaped traveller's self-writing should be among the questions we investigate and contexts we consider (Roberts 2012; Sau and Eissa-Barroso 2022).

The recent expansion and flourishing of the study of early modern life writing has had a relatively limited effect on the ways of studying travel writing prior to the Grand Tour. In the context of mobility and travel studies, questions of 'the self' or life writing have also been of little interest, apart from occasional efforts to excavate the backgrounds of travellers to include a short biography (e.g. 'X was born in Y to middling sort/gentry parents') in opening sections. Instead of a traveller's life and self, scholars of travel writing have more often explored travellers' authorship and rhetoric: their credibility and authority building, rhetoric of knowledge and race-making, and gaze towards foreignness and otherness, that is key questions of identity, power, and representation (Kuehn and Smethurst eds. 2015; Kamps and Singh 2001; Singh ed. 2009). I am not suggesting we turn our gaze away from these important questions, but rather, in addition to seeing travellers as travel writers and 'knowledge producers', that we also see them as life writers: writers of a significant, memorable, and curious mobile part of their own life, writing that took several forms from short personal notes to longer efforts to clear one's name, as authors who were very aware of how they were presenting themselves in their texts.[5] Usually the two general aims of knowledge production and life writing became entangled and difficult to fully separate; there is neither a need to separate these nor to get rid of advances already made. As I already mentioned, both are needed to understand these texts.

In one rare overview of the field, Simon Cooke presents a trajectory of travel writing beginning with Herodotus' *Histories*, which he terms as a search for an 'autobiographically inflected form of travel writing' (Cooke 2016). Cooke proceeds quite quickly to his own period of expertise, the eighteenth century, where he places the 'inward turn' in travel writing and consequently his own

---

[5] For a discussion on diaries, which 'record only a circumscribed period of time, usually related to a particular activity – a pilgrimage, military campaign, or sea-voyage.' See Stewart 2018.

focus. For example, Christopher Columbus, Francis Drake, and Walter Raleigh are quickly dismissed because 'the first-person self and its transformations through travel are not the focus of the account' (Cooke 2016, p. 16).

Similar to Cooke, the pioneering Dutch historian of autobiography and ego-documents, Rudolf Dekker, excluded several travel journals from his study of Dutch travel accounts. For inclusion in the study, 'the author had to write about his own experiences or provide personal commentary'; materials held in private collections were not taken into account; 'impersonal accounts', that is more schematic materials and guidebooks, were not admitted; and only accounts 'that were written on a personal initiative' were accepted (Dekker 1995, 278). It is important to recognise the differences in scope and purpose of the varied travel writings. However, sieving them to separate and qualify only the accounts with enough interiority and sensibility often leads to only studying the 'usual suspects' of travel writing, thus separating these texts from their contexts – as was the case with guidebooks and earlier printed accounts, which often significantly shaped single-authored travellers accounts by providing them with structure and subject matter alike (Enenkel and de Jong 2019; MacLean 2004a; Palmer 2011). We need to ensure that we facilitate revealing the specific ways that travel writings present a traveller, and for that we should not categorise too much beforehand.

Although often fluid or fluctuating, genre-boundaries can sometimes help to articulate differences in representations of the travelling and mobile self. Unlike scholars who have dismissed earlier travel writings from the fold of life writing, Zoë Kinsley has argued that travel writing has been too often and too easily conflated with autobiography (Kinsley 2014). Her analysis of eighteenth-century English women's accounts of their 'home tours' has demonstrated that a writer's relocation from home often invited more self-reflections than more familiar surroundings, a phenomenon we can still see at work (Kinsley 2014, p. 72). However, she also warns that if we expect early modern travel writing to always offer very clear 'autobiographical revelations', we are bound to be disappointed and should instead be mindful of the 'complex and varied nature of travelogues' (Kinsley 2014, p. 73). It has also been pointed out by Meredith Skura that if we judge early modern (travel) texts according to later conceptions of inwardness and reflexivity, much of it will inevitably fail the test of time and end up being left outside the remits of our studies (Skura 2008).

Travel accounts, of course, did more than merely describe the deeds of their authors and should not be read as less complex depictions of the 'travelling self' than memoirs or autobiographies. The travel accounts depict the alignment of early modern lives with others and with God; 'others' refer to intended readers and audiences and also subjects of commemoration in ways that emphasise the individual traveller less than is often expected from autobiographies. In addition, as social and relational texts, travel accounts show, and sometimes show off, the travellers' connections, contacts, friendships, and family relations due to serving multiple purposes for their authors. Some authors preferred publishing their accounts for a larger audience as an essential way of gaining useful contacts and attracting potential patrons, while other authors preferred circulating their accounts in manuscript form for either smaller coterie audiences or their friends and loved ones. The Elizabethan gentleman John North, illuminatingly studied by John Gallagher, used his manuscript diary to not only record his experiences of travel in Italy but also as a vehicle to maintain and fashion a cosmopolitan and multilingual identity, showing how travellers employed their travel experiences in their self-fashioning after their return (Gallagher 2017).

One of my case studies in this Element concerns seventeenth-century Cornish merchant traveller Peter Mundy (fl. 1597–1667), who wrote in his manuscript travel account *Itinerarium Mundii* that a large part of his life's journeys to the East had been performed in the service of others. In contrast, his travels in Britain and the Nordic countries were made to feed his own 'habituall disposition for travelling'. Stressing the benefits of keeping personal records, writing a travel account enabled Mundy to 'keepe my owne remembraunce on occasion off Discourse concerning particularities off thes voyages, As allsoe to pleasure such Friends (who might come to the reading thereof) Thatt are Desirous to understand somwhatt off Forraigne Countries' (Mundy 1907, p. 3). For Mundy, account writing, or in his case 'relation' writing, also became a lifelong project, which reveals how early modern travellers regarded their voyages as not just necessary to produce knowledge about the world, but also as life-changing personal experiences worthy to be commemorated and pinned down.

By now, I hope to have sufficiently stressed that if we judge early modern (travel) texts according to later conceptions of inwardness and reflexivity, much of it will inevitably fail the test of time and end up being left outside the remits of our studies. Travellers were active shapers of their accounts, recording their associated actions, thoughts, and motivations, aided by vast textual and cultural resources that helped them make sense of their travel experience, very often with hindsight after their travels had ended, and usually through a process of composition in which texts travelled between forms and genres, and were shaped and directed for diverse publics.[6] One key method of building credibility in travel writing was eyewitnessing by the traveller, who performed and wrote about their own journey, and their other senses, as will be more fully discussed in the next section.

---

[6] A similar shaping process is visible in a wide range of 'autobiographical texts' in England (Smyth 2010).

Annoyingly, at least to a nosy and curious researcher of the embodied and emotional experiences of travellers, the early modern traveller's 'self' often manifests itself in very subtle ways, such as through omissions, light editions, and additions, or even strategic vagueness that sought to protect the traveller from harm in sensitive political situations, such as during wartime or when travelling through hostile territories (Holmberg 2017). In other circumstances, travellers partook and utilised common autobiographical strategies of presenting and framing themselves, developed further in family books, memoirs, spiritual autobiographies, and *vitae* of both saints and sinners, apologising for putting their pen to paper, justifying their actions, and dropping both strong and subtle hints at their presence in the events they described. These written mobile lives took many forms, as did their texts, and their occasional fragmentariness should not scare us off.

Travel accounts showed signs of their authors' autobiographical or 'life writing' in both simple and complex ways. In addition to the most well-known textual devices involving the early modern traveller-author being present and framing this presence (the preface, dedicatory epistles, epilogues, side notes, and edits), textual devices particular to travel writing were at their disposal and borrowed from other non-literary modes for the recording and description of the self. These textual devices included (but were not restricted to) financial accounting, logbooks, commonplace books, notes in almanacs, and personal notebooks. Such texts often gave very subtle hints at individual experience and agency and may have included either very short notes about sensory and embodied experiences (that were often placed in side notes or marginalia) or instances where the texts hinted at or revealed the processes of writing and commemoration. These themes will be tackled in the following sections with the help of short case studies and travellers' texts that lend themselves to examination from these angles.

In the three sections that follow, I aim to apply recent advances in early modern life writing studies to a cultural-historical investigation of early modern travel accounts in order to discover how the variety of modes of autobiographical recording and accounting were used in travel writing. Focusing on three somewhat overlapping themes (embodiment, materiality, and memory), I will show the contexts and themes that invited travellers to describe both their surroundings and their individual experiences.

2 Mediating Experience: The (Ailing) Body, Emotions, and Senses of the Traveller

Descriptions of bodily ailments and suffering were often the clearest markers of travellers' embodied presence in their writing. They also offered the clearest route to the autobiographical elements of travel writing – in addition to declarations of literary intent, purpose, and apologies for writing badly. These descriptions of very personal and often visceral embodied experiences could range from grief, languishing, and illness to descriptions of torture at the hands of the Inquisition or being beaten by ruffians on the road. They offer us many paths to explore travellers' autobiographical memory and the writing of their inner worlds during their travels.

Despite being ubiquitous, travellers' embodiment (and their non-ocular senses) has gained far less attention than travellers' eyewitnessing and gaze on foreign lands, making the travellers often somewhat disembodied witnesses to foreign lands and peoples. Consequently, eyewitnessing has also taken centre stage over travellers' other sensory experiences in histories of travel, knowledge, and science.[7] The focus has long been on the autoptic verification, knowledge-building, and credibility-enhancing aspects of travel writing, investigating its connections with the histories of science and scholarship, and the construction of geographic and ethnographic knowledge (Davies and Whitehead 2012; Hacke, Jarzebowski, and Ziegler 2021; Ord 2008; Rubiés 2000b; Tarantino and Zika 2019). Accordingly, emotional, sensory, or indeed multisensory experiences of mobility, such as ailing and illness or hallucination, have been seen as distortions or obstacles: they disrupt the gathering of travel knowledge or prevent the traveller from travelling, observing, and witnessing new worlds and have not been the focus of scholarship so far. There are notable exceptions to this, but there is definitely room for more work on travellers' inner worlds and experiences.[8]

The quintessential knowledge-building strategy we know to expect from early modern travel writing concerns eyewitnessing; but having it as the main focus has led us to pay insufficient attention to the rest of the sensorium – touch, taste, hearing, smell, and their multisensory and synaesthetic combinations – despite the existence of both direct and subtle references to these in archives (Jenner 2011). Suffering, illness, and travellers' descriptions of their embodied experiences can, however, be approached as an integral part of the traveller's self-writing and not just a method of verification or giving evidence that the traveller wrote about the things he or she had witnessed or felt (Sell 2012; Thompson 2007). In fact, I argue here that we cannot fully understand travel writing if we ignore traveller-writers in all their often messy, even gory embodiment by either skipping over these episodes or only mining them for juicy anecdotes. In many cases, especially when corrupted by foreign air or food, following Annemarie Mol's ideas, the traveller's stomach arguably participated in making knowledge just as much as their eyes, and we need to examine these

---

[7] There are some notable exceptions that explore travellers' sensory experiences, including Agnew 2012; Youngs 2019.

[8] Notable exceptions include Williams 2022.

moments more carefully, also paying more attention to their 'fashioning' of the traveller's suffering self (Mol 2021). As an example that will be explored further, illness descriptions were folded with other layers of the traveller's story: they allowed travellers to not only show fellow feeling for their ailing companions, gratitude for received hospitality at their own time of need, and an occasion to explain the extra costs and troubles their journeys had brought them, but also sometimes offered an occasion to drop hints to future patrons of much-needed support. Ailments also helped in keeping time; these personal embodied experiences of continuous threats to health and cyclical returns of illness helped to mark time (Newton 2018; Thorley 2016).

This section explores how travel and mobility invited the recording of the embodied experiences of the traveller, and how these experiences can be approached with the tools of life writing studies to inform our readings of embodiment and its functions in travel writing. Throughout the section, my readings of manuscripts and printed travel writings, concentrating mainly on the manuscript commonplace book and its published sections by Levant Company clerk John Sanderson (fl. 1584–1602), will be in dialogue with new histories of the senses, emotions, and medicine.[9] My aim is to consider travellers' embodied experiences as simultaneously affective, intimately entangled, and multisensory and explore how these experiences participated in the writing of the travelling self (Smith 2015).

Embodied experiences of illness and grief were often both sensory and emotional, and in this way, were tied to the commemorative impulses and aims of self-description and life writing: if sufficiently visceral and memorable, they became events. Purpose, context, and form shaped their expression and recording, not only at home but also abroad. My explorations of the representations of bodily experiences of illness and ailing are tied to the construction and fashioning of the ailing and (usually) heroic self of the traveller. Travellers, if they lived to tell the tale, usually survived their illness as a result of connections, providence, and resourcefulness and were consequently compelled to acts of commemoration and gratitude. Experiences of illness, death, and survival during travels, and the ways in which travellers sought to preserve and express their embodied experiences, ranged from subtle hints at not only sight and hearing, that is eye- and ear-witnessing, but also to taste, touch, and smell, which combined in descriptions of ailing and illness. Their embodied nature caused them to become evocative, dramatic, and effective warnings to future travellers, fulfilling the needs of both didacticism and self-fashioning (Holmberg 2021).

---

[9] See BL Lansdowne MS 241, the diary and common place book of John Sanderson. For convenience, the Hakluyt edition is cited here; the following references will be to the pages of this edition instead of the manuscript. See Sanderson 1931.

Illness abroad could be a life-threatening (just as much as it was life-changing) event, which not only complicated foreign travels but also gave cause to recording the illness for posterity. Whether life-threatening or just annoying, it added to the hardship and costs of travel and required explanations for lost goods or rerouting, and called for both hospitality and gratefulness towards generous hosts and interlocutors who saved the day. Similar to pain, illness qualifies as an event that required comprehension, justification, explanation, and gratitude in the case of recovery (Bourke 2017). Like any other life-changing events, illnesses were worth noting down for the benefit of the (past and future) traveller, their families and relations, and readers further afield. This type of recording for the benefit of self and others explains why serious illnesses were written down, not only in travel writings but also in early modern life writings of all kinds, ranging from travel texts to family books, from commonplace books to memoirs and recipe books, where cures and recipes were both recorded for those who stayed at home and slipped into records that were meant to accompany the traveller (Leong 2013; Rankin 2016). Travelling was a dangerous business in this period, not entered into lightly and without thorough preparation. In fact, many authors mention that before setting off on their travel, they had wagered upon their return as a form of financing their travel, a common custom at the time, or only after making a will (Parr 2012).

Literature on medical advice to travellers was relatively scarce, which resulted in dedicated health advice to travellers often being scattered in the medical literature from antiquity to the Renaissance (Horden 2005). The alchemist, physician, and itinerant scholar Guglielmo Gratarolo's (1516–1568) *Iter Agentium* was one of the few pieces of advice available during this time. However, this advice was never translated into English, probably because the market was already saturated by more general advice, and travellers already knew where to seek it: travel books or their own associates for face-to-face or epistolary or 'guidance', which required adaptation to specific climates and persons (Cavallo and Storey 2017). Travel writings in both manuscript and print included not only descriptions of symptoms and guesses at causes but also some advice on how to both prevent and cure illness when far from home. In these episodes, foreign lands attack the body of the traveller – making it imperative for the traveller to adapt to foreign airs, waters, and places. They also had to pay more attention to the building blocks of early modern health known as the 'six non-natural things', that is air, food and drink, rest and exercise, sleep and waking, excretions and retentions (coitus), and mental affections, all more difficult to control while on the move and away from home, familiar foods, and loved ones (Earle 2014). Quite often, as in the case of John Sanderson, illnesses were significant milestones on the journey through life, which were recorded as life events, among the many other annoyances, obstacles, and hardships of life abroad.

John Sanderson's Life's Ailments and Censures

The early modern archive of travels in the Levant is rich in sensory and embodied experiences of travellers, and this is true especially of their varied illnesses and ailments that were rife in the near and far East alike. Most English travellers and traders of the early modern period knew about the potential risks to life and limb, ranging from dysentery to plague and fevers, and John Sanderson – a 'factor' (i.e. representative) and clerk of the Levant Company between the years 1584 and 1602 – was no exception. We will encounter Sanderson and his travels in the Levant later in this Element as well, but for now, we will focus on the contribution of illnesses to accidents, calamities, and ill fortunes that Sanderson recorded not only for posterity but possibly first and foremost for himself.

Sanderson first travelled to Istanbul in 1584 as a young man of twenty-four. This was a time when the English trade and diplomatic relations with the Ottoman sultan were still in their infancy – syndicate trading with the Ottomans was chartered on 11 September 1581 (Mather 2009; Wood 1964). Sanderson has left us an unusually strong paper trail of personal writings and documents, all rich sources for the social and cultural historian of mobility and travel writing alike. His writings comprise not only letters and correspondence but also some accounts and notes in a commonplace book fashion. In addition to this material and within the pages of this same 'commonplace book', Sanderson wrote both a short autobiography and a manuscript account of his travels and dealings in the Levant; long extracts of the manuscript were later published in Samuel Purchas' famous collection of travel narratives, the monumental *Purchas His Pilgrimes* in 1625. Unusually for Purchas' sources, we can compare the versions of Sanderson's accounts in manuscript and print and interpret the varied meanings of what was edited, what was excised, and what was left for the eyes of not the many but the few (Holmberg 2021c).

In the short autobiographical section of his manuscript (entitled 'a record of the birthe and fortunes of John Sanderson, alias Bedic'), Sanderson recorded both his 'censures' and the many trials of his life, a practice familiar to many a Puritan and Presbyterian author (Capp 2019; Lynch 2012). However, at least at face value, Sanderson's 'record' was more focused on life-threatening illnesses and escapes from the claws of death than on spiritual trials, with self-chastisement and efforts at reform added only later as comments. Sanderson writes that he was a sickly child from infancy, whose schoolmasters beat him up regularly, leaving both visible and invisible scars (Sanderson 1931, pp. 1–2). Sanderson's practice of naming his ill-behaved family members, supposedly badly behaved apprentices, and other wrongdoers hints that his account was not intended for print publication and that it was written from a very particular yet often elusive perspective. The practice of restricted manuscript publication and recording was not unheard of: authors often circulated their writings in manuscript to keep records of family events, accidents, births, and deaths, or to ensure their version of events was heard (Marschke 2022).[10] Other people, be they family or colleagues, became foils for Sanderson. Like his many illnesses, they disrupted the flow of his life, some causing longer suffering and pain than others. One of the few positive descriptions of a living being in Sanderson's text was of his horse, a 'Babilonian', which he remembers 'would walke by me, licking my hand; stand still when I backed him; and kneele at my pleasure' (Sanderson 1931, pp. 14–15).

After his arrival in the Levant, Sanderson's illnesses punctuated the daily rhythms of trade and diplomacy that he probably considered too mundane or unnecessary to record in greater detail. Arriving in Istanbul in 1584, the ambassador William Harborne had made Sanderson the 'maister of his howse', where he, to his great grief, 'remained in that sort six monethes' and reported that during this time he 'was daingerously sicke at one time, but sone recovered' (3). More dangerously still, for the next eighteen months, Sanderson was sent to plague-ridden Cairo to manage the Turkey Company business. There he claims to have counted the deaths of at least 'two hundred in a day at Cairo', in addition to the many others who died at 'Alexandria and at Rossetto', which served the purpose of both reporting on the dangers of foreign lands, and perhaps his own bravery and providence guarding him against illness (4–5).[11] This kind of intelligence gathering about illness in foreign lands was expected from travellers, but in Sanderson's life story, they take on the additional function of aiding his time-keeping by noting all memorable events and accidents during his stay. When separated by time and distance from home,

---

[10] The life writings of one Alice Thornton served to clear her name and resolve a conflict over family property ownership (Edge 2023).

[11] Sanderson's brushes with the plague continued both in Aleppo, which was at that time the centre of Middle Eastern trade, and in Istanbul, which was a regular hub of the disease during the sixteenth and seventeenth centuries. In the latter, Sanderson reports that the 'plague of pestelence was also in the ambassiators [Edward Barton's] house' [in Istanbul] and that 'Sixteen had it in a short time; eight died, one of which (Starkie by name) sickned in my chamber in the night time [and] died two or three dayes after,' again marking down both providential and lucky escapes from death. See Sanderson 1931, pp. 12–13. Even if Sanderson's record here is far from Daniel Defoe's *The Journal of the Plague Year*, he took part in early modern 'plague writing' in this small way.

travellers employed a great variety of methods of keeping and measuring time (Williams 2022).

With all the risks involved in foreign travel, it was not uncommon for travel texts to paint the traveller as either exceptionally lucky, blessed, or tenacious to have escaped illness and epidemics throughout their travels, especially if these were long and took them far away from their homeland. Public-facing texts could also boast of such feats. Traveller Thomas Coryate wrote about his invincible health from India, where he would later die, saying that 'in all my travels since I came out of England, I have enjoyed as sound a constitution of body, and firme health, as ever I did since I first drew this vitall ayre libertie, strength of limbs, agilitie of foot-manship', not a mean feat trundling around the Levant, Persia, and India, which were considered notoriously unhealthy and dangerous for Western visitors (Coryate 1616, p. 4).[12]

For Sanderson, the plagues of Cairo served to show his own fearlessness, allowing him to fashion himself as a Levant traveller of true grit and courage, and most of all, perhaps, being a man of experience and expertise to whom the less experienced could turn to for advice, also later in life. Sanderson reported seeing dead bodies daily, both lying on the streets and washing up on land, writing that nonetheless, he did not fear for his life, and that he 'had no want of health, though the country is tediouse in respect of heate, dust, and flies' (Sanderson 1931, p. 4). Such complaints were common among the early modern travellers, who feared that their bodies would struggle to acclimatise (Kupperman 1984). Early modern health regimens strived for the stability and balance of 'humours', temperatures, and diets. Also of importance was the knowledgeable management of the six non-natural things, this is a specic early modern concept, not an element – air, food and drink, exercise and rest, sleep and wakefulness, excretion and retention, and passions of the mind – the foremost determinants of health and well-being that influenced human bodies from the outside. Complications of this management involved the adjustment and adaptation of all six elements to travellers' individual complexions, their unique combinations of elemental and humoral qualities, and maintenance of their healthy balance (Gentilcore 2016; Stolberg 2011).

To document not only his tenacity but also his loyalty and trustworthiness, Sanderson remarked that neither pestilence nor shipwreck had prevented him from fully carrying out his duties, and that he had managed to avoid any extra

---

[12] On page 31, Coryate adds that he is still enjoying 'as pancraticall and athleticall a health as euer I did in my life', apart from three days in Constantinople, where he suffered from an 'ague' [a fever or shivering fit], which was quickly cured by bloodletting. See also Coryate 1611, where Coryate reports on suffering from seasickness, which is depicted in the frontispiece as well. According to Edward Terry, Coryate died in Surat of a flux, which was aggravated by the drinking of 'sack' offered to him by Englishmen (Terry 1655, p. 76).

losses to the Levant Company beyond some 'provision of wood, wine, and houshold stufe'. It seems that one of the purposes of Sanderson's text was to safeguard himself against accusations of corporate losses and perhaps prevent later lawsuits against him. If calamities such as the plague affected the Company's trade, it was better to keep a record to which Sanderson could turn if needed. He also kept tally of other things: a list of the many troubles his apprentice caused him and a record of the (often sorry) fates of his enemies.[13] Similarities can be found in printed travel writing, albeit often in more candid and shrouded form: to defend, attack enemies, or seek compensation and retaliation. In the case of suffering and loss of life, a traveller naturally wanted to attract pity, compassion, and potential new patrons if illness struck them down.[14]

Upon his arrival in Tripoli in present-day Lebanon, another life-threatening 'illness event' caught up with Sanderson, which he described as 'beinge safely and in perfect health arived, after a while I fell greviously sick,' a line very similar to other contemporary markings in diaries of ailing people. Sanderson also notes that he had been 'sowinge a little gould in my doblett (for the next day I should have gone for Alepo, my horse hire paid for and aparell sent)' (Sanderson, 1931, p. 5). Eerily, Sanderson had felt a 'paulpable blowe one the left shoulder, which staied me [on] my asse', when he had been riding one evening at the waterside together with a janissary, despite neither of them having seen where the blow had come from. Sanderson here paints a vivid scene where his illness strikes him down dramatically and out of the blue – as illnesses were often thought to do to their helpless sufferers, corresponding to the hand of God, striking down sinners or Saul on his way to Damascus.[15] The only difference concerns the lack of consequent spiritual transformation or conversion, and the eerie ambiguity about the supernatural nature of the event.

Upon arriving in his chambers, Sanderson 'soncke downe' on his lute, breaking it into pieces, informing us at the same time of his musical pursuits (Sanderson 1931, pp. 4–5). After recovering a little and creeping to the door, he managed to shout for help and some 'aqua-vita', after which he 'threwe' himself 'thawart the bed' (Sanderson 1931, pp. 4–5). The course and identity of Sanderson's illness remains vague, but he describes being bedridden for quite some time. Like many of his fellow English travellers in the Levant, Sanderson

---

[13] 'Yet had I no feare at all, nor failed to frayght a barke to carie me and the Companies goods for Tripolie [in] Sirria … ' See Sanderson, 1931, 4–5.

[14] An example of this is the case of William Lithgow's sufferings at the hands of the Spanish Inquisition (Lithgow 1632). For Lithgow's books, see Bosworth 2006.

[15] For narratives of children falling ill, see Newton 2011.

suspected the cause might have been the 'corrupted' air of Tripoli that had infected not just himself but the forty to fifty Englishmen residing there at the time. The noxious and 'miasmatic' air was feared by many Levant Company men conducting trade in Syria and Aleppo, the trading hub connecting the overland routes between the Levant and India (Linte 2022; Pannel 2017). Discussions of diseases having various causes, corrupting their stomachs or striking them down with fevers, lurked in the middle of their accounts.[16]

Sanderson's illness at this time was so severe that he claimed 'everyone' was convinced of his imminent death; indeed, a coffin had been made for him.[17] These kinds of claims are common in illness narratives: sometimes letters are sent back home to worried relatives before news arrives about the patients' recovery, or the traveller arrives home much altered, correcting premature news of their death (Frank 1995).

Similar to other illness narratives, which punctuated the authors' account of their lives, survival from illness abroad was not only a testament to a traveller's tenacity but, especially when explained by providence, comparable to illnesses in other forms of life writing such as the spiritual autobiography, diary, family book, or memoir (Thorley 2016, pp. 42–3). The providentialism of much of early modern life-writing provided a shared language in which to wrap stories of illness abroad and warn future travellers about all the possible dangers threatening unprepared novices and seasoned traders alike. These moments of ailing, death, and survival depicted in travellers' writings illustrate their purpose not just as concerning their travels and pursuits of knowledge but also themselves, in all their humoral and emotional messiness. Hardship made life events memorable and not just profitable.[18]

When explaining his slow recovery, jaundice, and constant swooning if forced to sit upright, Sanderson noted that he was eventually cured after being ill for four months. During his illness, he consumed barley porridge, chicken broth, and 'stewed' (boiled) prunes and apricots with their juice. These were common medications for ailments of the stomach, including dysentery or so-called 'fluxes', considered sufficiently gentle foods to be recommended to ailing patients, regardless of where in the world they were (Sanderson 1931, p. 5).[19] More well-known places for such notes were recipe books, in which (mostly) women recorded their own changing diets and cures and those of their loved

---

[16] Tripoli had been recently adopted as the new harbour for English Levant trade due to costs that had made the equally notorious and unhealthy former harbour, Iskenderun, less popular.

[17] 'That Tripoli ayre at that time had infected 40 or 50 Inglishmen at least. Onely the maisters mate and four others died. The coffin was made and sett out for me, but God prevented that busines (His name be ever praised).' (Sanderson 1931, p. 5).

[18] The same logic seemed to work in plague-writing. See Rolfe 2020.

[19] For curative diets and gentle foods, see Newton 2015.

ones, sometimes also noting changes in their scenery and cooking.[20] Travel writings rarely resemble recipe books, although it is not unheard of, as we can see here as well as in Fynes Moryson's *Itinerary*, where the formerly ailing traveller recommends his own failed regimen to stay healthy during travels. Noticing connections between other forms like these helps us appreciate the richness of travel writing even more, and how it relied on the experience, expertise, and self-presentation of the traveller (Leong 2013; Rankin 2016).

A final illness Sanderson suffered from in the Levant, during his stay in Aleppo, for which he recommended neither a simple cure nor a recipe, was 'tenasmose', a form of constipation which John Florio's '*Vocabolario Italiano and Ingelese*' defines as 'a great desire to go often to the stool, and be able to do nothing' (Florio 1611, p. 416). Using the opportunity to note some experiential knowledge, Sanderson interpreted his 'tenasmose' as being caused by his own refusal to take 'phisique', here probably meaning a light purgative, 'according to the costome, to prevent sicknes', perhaps unwisely going against received wisdom and health advice he had received.[21] He also mentioned that ambassador Edward Barton was at this time 'sicke of a flux,' perhaps connecting his own illness to the ambassador's more serious dysentery. Sanderson seems to have thought that his 'tenasmose' was caused by something else entirely, which explained his refusal to accept the most common cure. Writing it down in his commonplace book might have served the purpose of warning both future travellers Sanderson might advise or show it to and, as my hunch is, keeping a record of his own ailments, perhaps anticipating their return one day.

Problems with the stomach such as Sanderson's constipation, diarrhoeas, and especially the feared dysentery or 'bloody flux', were all well-known diseases for the English Levant travellers, with dysentery probably being the most feared and dangerous of them all. By the time Sanderson was writing his account, after his return to England, dysentery had claimed the life of Sanderson's boss, ambassador Edward Barton, on 28 February 1598. It had also seriously plagued Thomas Roe's residence in India, making several returns (Das 2023). Several other unnamed men who left their homeland for the riches and opportunities offered by trade and colonisation were recorded in ship's logs, trading company correspondence, and the margins of travel accounts, either according to their death or suffering from similar diseases (Hubbard 2021, pp. 172–3).

---

[20] For example, Lady Anne Fanshawe's recipe books started recording local recipes when her family moved to Spain. See Fanshawe 1651–1707. For the recipe book project, see the Early Modern Recipes online project's website.

[21] Sanderson probably refers to a light purgative, although 'physic' could also mean medicine in general. See 'physic, n.' OED Online.

Other mobile English lives cut short by dysentery included traveller-author Fynes Moryson's younger brother Henry Moryson in 1597, and traveller-author Thomas Coryate, who had earlier boasted of his invincible health but finally succumbed to the 'flux' during his travels in India in 1617. Sanderson might have feared the same fate as these men when he refused to be purged by the Venetian consul's doctor, insisting that his problems were caused by something else than 'the evell aire and change of waters, with the Turks spongie sower bread and rawe frutes', showing his familiarity with contemporary fears about food, although he refused to believe they were the causes of his own illness:

> But I ether toke it in a cupp of rosasolas the night before I departed frome the ambassiator, or else it was 400 d[uca]ts gould which I caried quilted in my purple velvett doblett, that all the way in ridinge beat uppon the raines of my backe. Be it howsoever, both strange, very painefull, and daingierouse the deseace was to me. Yet, I thanke God, in three monthes I was well recovered, and went to Siprus in the Navi Ragazona, John Douglas pilot, myselfe, G. Dorry[ng]ton, Alex. Harris, and Antony Marlo passingers. (Sanderson 1931, pp. 15–16)

Sanderson tried to make sense of his illness with the help of both prevailing medical knowledge and his own experience, claiming that he had contracted the disease from a glass of 'rosasolas' – or from his own money purse hitting him on the back.[22] As we have already seen elsewhere, with the incident on horseback, Sanderson was prone to magical thinking and thus could have also connected his illness to avarice. Be that as it may, Sanderson demonstrated in many passages how his obstinate views and sharp tongue got him into trouble with his closest colleagues and might thus have resisted listening to their advice as well (Holmberg 2021b; Holmberg 2022).

Reporting on contagious and dangerous illnesses was expected from travel writers of both public-facing and more privately circulating accounts. Travel books and manuscripts were supposed to gather intelligence, construct knowledge from many angles, and give aid to all those who sought to 'plant' themselves in newly established colonies and trading centres abroad. Instead of scaring off their readers, a public-facing traveller-author was expected to describe 'the generall well-faring of the inhabitants', counting the absence of endemic diseases among the natural resources and commodities of lands (Palmer 1606, pp. 82–3). The more personal this knowledge was, the more useful it was considered, and here lies the wider cultural relevance of many such

---

[22] This seems to have been a cordial made of sundew (*rosa solis*), of which Sanderson says to have drunk 'in my owne chamber, before I slept ... at least (for good respect) a bottell all out of rosasolas, of a pint (I say) at least, to prevent the wourst.' It was recommended for both consumption and as a laxative. Sanderson 1931, p. 15.

descriptions. More personally, Sanderson continued to advise and report on illness to his friends via his correspondence, while his autobiography had kept a more personal tally and record of the calamitous illnesses of his own life.[23] Due to the rarity of such embodied experiences among the vast majority of Englishmen of his times, Sanderson's experience was of value not only to himself, helping to avoid and cure future ailments, but also to prevent and warn those without similar experiences.

Throughout his short autobiography, Sanderson threaded his life's illnesses into his travels in the Levant and to all the other mischiefs and annoyances of his life. In his manuscript commonplace book, Sanderson's perspective on both his own life and his illnesses was autobiographical, commemorative, and retrospective: he noted down his experiences after returning to England as further reference and a record of his life events. Back home, he attributed his recoveries to both God's mercy and miraculous cures, but he left vague the causes of his illnesses, probably expecting to fill in some blanks later on when he had more access to expert knowledge and books. Even if Sanderson sometimes seemed to eschew prevailing medical knowledge, he also recorded recipes and remedies in his manuscript, even adding to an index to the end of his manuscript to help him recover information when needed. We have recently come to appreciate recipe books and family books as rich repositories of both biographical and autobiographical information and elements familiar from life writing elsewhere, and this appreciation also applies to Sanderson's writings. The richness of Sanderson's own travel archive is a testament to both his travels and how he wrote his life around his embodied experiences of mobility and the many sufferings these had caused him. In his account of his mobile life, his body literally took centre stage, expressing tenacity, providence, and bravery, and his hard-earned travel knowledge and experiences throughout, documenting both ailing and recovery along the way.

Suffering Heat, Cold, Hunger, and Thirst: Environment, the Senses, and the Traveller

Travellers were physically present in their texts, not only when their bodies were unwell, although these situations were the most dramatic and visible instances of their 'embodiedness' being on show. Travellers' senses and emotions participated in recording their travel experiences, and as I argue here, contributed to the writing and fashioning of themselves in their texts, whether ailing or healthy. In situations when feeling hunger, thirst, or heat and cold, travellers were able to show (and even show off) their embodied experiences

---

[23] For the connectedness of travelogues, diaries, and letters, see Kinsley 2019.

and hard-earned knowledge on how to survive. In this process, they used their own bodies both to construct and demonstrate their knowledge and express themselves as knowledge-builders; a process that often resembled later constructions of scholarly personae, a practice amongst scholars that has never really ceased but only changed shape and methods to become less embodied (Featherstone 2019, pp. 1–19).

We can also notice the presence of the sensing and emoting traveller in several contexts, such as touching stones, smelling the air, and making judgments about foreign foods. The history of the senses and emotions has offered more tools for us to approach these episodes, but I argue that these tools work even better when combined with both social and cultural historical readings of the meanings such descriptions had in these accounts and, again, viewing them as writing the full (embodied) lives of the traveller (Swann 2018).

Until very recently, emotions and senses in travel writing were mainly explored for their 'ethnographic' functions: analysing the traveller's representation and (eye-) witnessing of foreign lands, foreigners, and their emotional composition as part of their otherness or uncivility, or the sensory experiences of alterity produced by sounds, sights, and interpretations of the lower sensorium, the uncivility of foodways, or biting hostility of harsh climates (Broomhall 2016; Ballantyne and Burton 2005; Davis 2002; Murphy 2021). Contrastingly, my focus is on the travelling and mobile sensing and emoting persona of the traveller; the travellers' 'subjective', yet very much cultural, experience of mobility. This type of experience is something that has often been claimed as either inaccessible to the historian, at least in any authentic or unfashioned form, or very rarely represented in the first place (Holmberg 2019; Ord 2008).

However, as with many phenomena studied in detail, the more a lens is focused, the more material is found. With more focus placed directly on their sensory experiences, early modern travellers suddenly appear in more sensory and emotional fullness than before, revealing themselves as not only eyewitnesses but also as ear-witnesses to sounds, as tasters of foods, as touchers of bodies and objects, and as smellers of both aromas and pungent smells, with diverse motives for writing such experiences down (Agnew 2012; Murphy 2021). Travellers come to the fore, touching, tasting, and otherwise feeling and sensing their surroundings and people and things they come across. This change can be explained not only as part of a move towards empirical witnessing in the early modern period and reporting on foreign lands in more systematic ways but also as having a long-standing tradition in classical rhetoric and narratives of pilgrimage, inviting emotional reactions from their readers and evoking their presence in the places they describe. Christian pilgrims sought to experience holy places both materially and virtually, imagining themselves partaking in the passion of Christ, visiting the Holy Sepulchre or faraway important sites and shrines, trying to taste the bitterness he had tasted and feel the sufferings he had felt.[24] Protestant travellers often struggled in trying to find a middle way, where they could visit the same sites though at the same time distancing themselves from Catholic practices (O'Donnell 2009).

Sensory experiences often intersected with descriptions of illness, but also the daily practices of feeding and taking care of the body. Travellers such as Henry Blount and Fynes Moryson reported on their sensory experiences entangled with their withered bodies and corrupted stomachs. They tasted the waters of the Danube and perhaps the Nile, and failed to eat and consume anything else than dried meat because their bodies had been ravaged by grief and corrupted by foreign airs, waters, and places (Din-Kariuki 2023). Others, such as William Lithgow, viscerally reported how their bodies were assaulted by foreign bandits, unsuitable or unwholesome foods, or the sheer lack of victuals – the stress of such descriptions of sensory phenomena was more often on things that went wrong than experiences that were smooth and untroubled.[25] A recurring theme was the struggle with the change in climate and foods, and the missing of usual customs and routines, at least after the novelty of travelling had worn off. Underlying all this was the worry that residing in foreign lands could inevitably and unalterably change the traveller, or quite simply kill him.

As if trying to convince himself that the Levant had not changed him, the travelling Levant Company chaplain William Biddulph wrote to a friend that he was 'weary of this uncomfortable Country' but that

> ... although I am now many thousand miles distant from you, yet I have changed but the aire, I remaine still the same man, and of the same minde, according to that old verse, though spoken in another sense, Coelum, non animos mutant qui trans mare currant. That is, They that over the sea from place to place doe passe, Change but the aire, their minde is as it was (Biddulph 1609).

Hiding beneath the surface of this wish was the troubling idea that residing for a long time in a foreign country could indeed change a man, both inside and out, both through a change in climate and through the new foods he was forced to consume (Earle 2014). It was feared that this might interfere not only with travellers' sensory and emotional makeup but also change something deeper within.

Historians used to struggle with the ephemerality of sensory experience, worrying about emotions and senses in history (Rosenwein 2002), and the

---

[24] See Beebe 2014 and her new project The Meaning of Virtual Pilgrimage in the Middle Ages.

[25] Lithgow famously reported on his suffering under torture and capture by the Spanish Inquisition and on being severely attacked by bandits in Cyprus. See Lithgow 1614: sig. F1v–F2.

ways they used to be studied either ahistorically or rigidly, or perhaps just too carelessly. However, nowadays we have a rich toolbox available to tease out the emotional and sensory experiences of the past, including the meanings of the whiffs of its smells (Dugan 2011; Tullett 2023). When studying the embodied and sensory experiences of travellers, employing these tools requires additional sensitivity to both mobility and the surrounding ephemerality of evidence: the awareness of the inescapable losses that have occurred regarding the props and paraphernalia of travel, and the difficulties of tying the experiences of singular travellers to the changing material contexts and objects, sceneries and land-scapes, ships, roads, and inns, employing interdisciplinary approaches of not only sensory history but of material culture studies as well.[26] Exciting avenues are being explored via studies of the spatiality of travel, the practices of mobility on early modern waterways and roads, and logistics. The destinations and locales of mobility and cultural encounters have also been explored, extending the range of protagonists of travel from the elites to those who moved due to their profession, war, or exile (Midura 2021). The next step should be to consider the experience of all this movement and the subsequent effects on culture, both to the people who moved and those who did not, and to read the discursive evidence in light of the surrounding materialities of travel. However, this does not mean forgetting about the intertextualities and self-fashioning functions of travel writing. The many rhetorical layers and mediations of sensory experiences continue to require sensitivity and nuance from readers, along with knowledgeability of genre and processes of writing; however, these are required for all writing in this period and should not prevent us from trying to explore these questions (Din-Kariuki 2023).

As in illness, the sensing body of the traveller most often emerges when either put in the 'wrong' climate for their humoral complexion or in a radically different environment, the effects of which were an enduring worry for early modern travellers, pilgrims, and colonisers alike (Kupperman 1984). Senses seemed to be heightened and observations sharpened by being in a strange and unfamiliar environment (Pettinger and Youngs 2020). It was usually the cross-ing of (bodily) boundaries, the need to control and cure the body, or the added cost that put both bodies and their embodied experiences in starker relief in travel writings of the time. When put in a climate that was not thought to be amenable to health – unlike, say, a spa (Corens 2022) – where the climate was considered either too cold or too hot, the air too unhealthy and miasmatic to an

---

[26] In this the new histories of mobility can help, placing the travellers and other mobile peoples more firmly in their localities, seeking the connections between 'locals', visitors, and immi-grants. See Zenobi 2021; Salzberg 2023; Sweet 2017.

individual traveller's complexion, travellers had to ask themselves how they would need to conduct themselves to survive.

As a sign of these worries, early modern travellers collected and wrote down recipes to cure and rebalance their bodies, read suitable health advice in advance, and noted warning examples of people who had been startled or surprised by such sudden changes. Rumours spread that some people had even died due to extreme heat or cold, with their bodily fat melting in the burning sun or their noses falling off in the extreme cold (Kupperman 1984). Merchant-traveller Peter Mundy, who we shall encounter again in the next section, recounted a story of being dangerously close to losing his fingers and nose due to extreme cold he suffered in Poland. This situation was all due to Mundy's own behaviour: he had decided to try how little clothing one needed in a snowstorm – similar experiences abound of other travellers in the North, ranging from Italian priests to French doctors exploring Scandinavia, or from the well-documented and researched Britons tragically failing in their search for the North-West passage (Fuller 2008; Mundy 2010, pp. 97–8; Raunio 2019). Travellers such as Mundy, Blount, and others used their own bodies to measure and test foreign lands, which resulted in more exciting narratives as well, unless things went wrong.

At the other end of the spectrum, hot climes were feared just as much as cold ones, even if English people of the time considered themselves as coming from the 'north' (Rubiés 2017). The long-suffering professional writer William Lithgow, the author of *The Totall Discourse of Rare Adventures* (1632 and its many previous editions) had truly travelled with his stomach empty, and his travels made him suffer even more for his art. Lithgow's body not only had to endure gruelling torture at the hands of the Spanish Inquisition, but also other calamities and violations. He had a lot to say also about the dangerous foods, surroundings, and hot air of the Levant, which threatened the balance of his body so much that he kept himself emaciated to fight off corruptions and imbalance. At one point, Lithgow reports suffering so much from the heat in Alexandria that during the day, he and his French companions 'did nought but in a low roome, besprinckle the water vpon our selues, and all the night lye on the top or platforme of the house, to haue the ayre,' feelings familiar from contemporary summers scorched by climate change (Lithgow 1632, pp. 324–5).

Lithgow's fear did not come out of nowhere: he had adopted Renaissance cultural fears about strange foods and diets along with climate theories that delineated the benefits of temperate climes. He claimed to have seen how his fellow travellers dropped like flies in the heat. Their misfortune related to their other poor life choices, with an undercurrent of social and moral commentary tainting his prose, warning his readers against excessive eating and drinking in foreign lands, lest they succumbed to 'surfeiting' and overheating their stomachs. Such was the terrible fate his German travel companions suffered on their journey from Jerusalem to Cairo, where they began drinking too much alcohol (Lithgow 1632, pp. 301–5).

The hot climate and the tropics were much feared and still little-known during the early age of European expansion: there were rumours about people who had died because, in their heat-induced delirium, also known as 'calenture', they had jumped off ships thinking that the vast seas were inviting green fields (Kupperman 1984, pp. 172–3). The fear of heat was common in all parts of the world in which travellers ended up: it affected plans of colonisation, made colonisers worry about their failing crops, and caused travellers to fear literally melting away in the sun. The heat also made common diseases more dangerous and harder to cure, and the balancing act of maintaining the equilibrium of bodily fluids more vital: the wrong equilibrium might result in perishing or, at least, languishing.

The act of eating and drinking was another vital moment when the traveller's sensing body participated in constructing their mobile self. Bodies involved in tasting, feeling, eating, and drinking were in intimate contact with foreign lands and customs in very corporeal ways and offered opportunities to manifest cultural preferences, civility, and good manners, and also to fashion the traveller as having accumulated such knowledge and experiences the hard way (Forsdick 2019). Descriptions of food and drink drew boundaries between travellers and foreign phenomena, delineating danger and safety, and purity and danger, while also producing vital travel knowledge about what foods were safe to consume abroad, and how these differed from or bore similarities to those available at home (Winchcombe 2022). In different climes, eating and drinking became a question of not only the themes we have already encountered in the context of illness: affordability, politeness, and hospitality; but they could also mean the difference between life and death. These issues were tied tangibly and viscerally to the body of the traveller, along with their morality, tenacity, class, and diverse tastes. Some travellers clung onto what they had been taught suited their bodies, lugging homely foods long distances, or trying to accommodate their tastes to the foods and diets abroad, while simultaneously being appropriately disgusted or horrified or complimentary towards local customs and foodways.

However, well-prepared in the beginning, travellers often had to eat what was available – no matter how rotten, hot, or dry, or even if the food was completely unsuited for their own humoral constitution and sensibility. Likewise, travellers often had to forego favourite drinks according to what was available or alternatively refrain from drinking altogether. Additionally, cultural prohibitions and health advice in the Levant were often in tension, as we saw in the account of

Lithgow and his drinking travel companions, a fact that helped to accentuate Lithgow's own moderate ways, saving him from both robbery and disease.

In addition to their direct connection to health and diet, descriptions of food and extra provisions (especially in the context of illness) carried with them more opportunities to express gratitude to benefactors encountered on the road. These instances can be read as writings of the self, especially the travelling 'social' self and its connections to others. Travellers thanked others in their texts for having provided money or loans, places to stay and recover, and for offering them nutritious and restorative substances. These details enable the texts to reach out beyond travels in the past, making efforts to shape the future, just as we have come to expect from diaries and memoirs that aimed to record their author's perspective and viewpoint. The instances also offer information on travellers' sensory experiences, along with their sociability and connections during travels, which went beyond the verification of their accounts. These included instances where foods and waters were tasted, scents and miasmas were smelled, and beds and other commodities were touched. Vision and hearing were also present.

Due to their suffering finances, travellers often had to compromise on either the quality or quantity of their food. Often, travellers described jumping on the chance of getting good, fresh food or recommending that successive travellers acquire provisions before certain stretches of their journey – as when entering hot territories such as the desert. Such episodes gave traveller-authors the opportunity not only to give cost-estimates of these provisions, recommendations, and warnings against certain foods or their poor quality, but also to thank especially hospitable hosts. Such an attitude also worked in their favour, fashioning themselves as courteous, grateful, and appreciative guests, with good connections to the English safety nets abroad. On the other side of the coin were laments about inadequate inns – or as was the case in the Levant, complaints about barely liveable Ottoman *khans* and rocky terrains, which had the capacity to disrupt sleep or irritate the stomachs of the most well-worn traveller – naturally risking one's reputation as a sturdy and intrepid traveller who could endure almost anything. As we already know, travel made the diet and the air harder to balance; in addition, travel disrupted sleep and, whether due to constant travel or heat, could make the body of the traveller even more permeable to disease, and allow it to absorb noxious humours, pestilential air, and sub-par victuals (Earle 2014). Recording edibles, curatives, drinks, and other sustenance available served the purpose of not only knowledge-building, but these representations also constructed a story of the travellers' adaptability, tenacity, and sometimes courage when confronted with strangeness, deficiency, or scarcity, all the while recording their sensory engagements with foreign lands.

Touching and Tasting the Holy Land: John Sanderson's Journey to Jerusalem

Nested in John Sanderson's already-mentioned commonplace book was a travel account about his years in the Levant, where he admitted he had once gotten so drunk with 'rachie' [*raki*] that a travel companion had to push his fingers down his throat to cause him to vomit. This incident forced Sanderson to thank his companion for saving his life in this way – and for his decision to never drink again, at least in such quantities. The crafty Sanderson also noted the names of everyone who became drunk that night, showing how closely drunkenness was tied to morality and masculinity, but kept this story to himself when he offered his writings to Samuel Purchas for wider publication in his famous *Pilgrimes* collection.

Sanderson's material and sensory contact with the Levant did not end with illness, food, or drinking. He seemed to be an exceptionally sensory and tactile traveller, feeling his way through the Ottoman domains in the Holy Land, Greek islands, and the capital with its annoying Levant Company men. Protestants such as Sanderson (and Fynes Moryson before him) seemed to be both culturally and religiously drawn to the sights, sites, and sounds of the Levant, although they often sought to find new ways to engage with the places that had been earlier destinations of Christian pilgrimages.

Sanderson's manuscript gives a sense that before his journey back to England in 1601, he had but one more thing to cross off his to-do list: a visit to Jerusalem. Sanderson departed from Istanbul on 14 May 1601 and arrived in Sidon on 3 June, where he joined a caravan of Jews heading to Jerusalem. Samuel Purchas later mentioned that his main reason for including Sanderson's travel account in his *Pilgrimes* was 'his pilgrim's' association with the Jews, something that would have been unusual and exotic in the contemporary climate of anti-Jewish sentiment in England. In Sidon, Sanderson struck up a deal with Jewish merchants and joined their caravan that was due to pass through the Holy Land to Jerusalem and back towards Aleppo. The generous Jews promised to make extra stops on the way to enable their Christian companion to visit the most revered places of his religion. On the journey, Sanderson mentions seeing Christians touching holy places, carving their names in stone. Seeming unsure of the correct way to conduct himself, Sanderson writes that he carved his own name only once, in a cave where Lazarus was supposed to have been buried, and that he also 'washed [his] hands and head and dranke of the river [Jordan] in divers places' (Sanderson 1931, p. 105, 113).

Sanderson's recordings of his life and travels are remarkable in the fullness of their representations of his embodiment and sensory experiences. They ranged from the meticulous recording of his ailments and illnesses to noting how he experienced foreign lands with his whole sensorium, touching the famous sites of

Jerusalem, smelling the corrupted airs of Tripoli, tasting the 'spongie bread' of the Turks, and hearing the sounds of the prayers of both Jews and Christians, along with the foul words and physical scuffles with his own compatriots in Istanbul. Despite being both deeply culturally and materially shaped by the commonplace book form and the demands of Sanderson's professional life, these experiences had deeply personal meanings to Sanderson, prompting him to record them distinctly, warts and all. Writing down the trials and most significant events of his own life and times in the Levant, some of Sanderson's motivations were somewhat muddied by Samuel Purchas' intrusive editorial work and mediation, but they still reveal a man with two faces and experiences: one he was willing to reveal to his closest friends in all its embodiedness, and one he was happy to fashion and advertise to the reading public of English travel writing.

In the next section, we will turn our gaze to the visual and textual forms and processes in which travellers wrote their experiences, and how these experiences were shaped by the habits of life writing, or in some cases, drawing.

3 Recording Material Mobile Lives

Inspired by recent work on both material texts, used (and annotated) books, and life-writing, this section takes on the challenge of interpreting travellers' recorded lives, which are embedded and fashioned in manuscripts in diverse textual and material forms (Sherman 2010; Smyth 2018; Stewart 2008; Stewart 2018). In this section, I argue that traces of travellers' life- or self-writing often resided somewhere beyond or alongside the 'main text': it could be found in ephemeral sources such as flyleaves, recipe books carrying remedies for the ailing and the seasick, and in the almanacs and notebooks recording both intentions and failed travel plans. 'Life-writing' could also be found, loosely defined, in the way text, objects, and images were put together as a collection, as if reinvented as material outcomes of the travellers' mobility (Nunn 2020). Further traces of travellers' mobile lives lurk in many places: in archives and court records, and in 'material texts' that do not at first glance seem to contain much about either travels or life writing, as demonstrated by recent work on early modern record-keeping practices and confessional mobility (Corens, Peters, and Walsham 2016; Corens 2016; Corens 2018; Corens 2022).

As we have learned from scholars of material texts, accounts of both lives and travels were often based on earlier notes in 'wastebooks' or other kinds of notebooks and later developed via several stages of editing and copying.[27]

---

[27] A waste book was a rough form of account book, where notes were jumbled up in a relatively disorganised manner, see Beal 1993. Thanks to the *Art of Travel 1500–1800* database, we can search a great variety of *ars apodemicae* for advice on note-taking and composition. See https://artoftravel.nuigalway.ie.

Just as Adam Smyth found in English church wardens' records and financial account books, life-writing and written mobile lives can be found in unexpected places, and often travelled between textual forms, showing signs of processing and editing in between (Smyth 2010). Likewise, travel writing usually traversed across different media from initial notes to the final accounts that were revised, edited, and more polished, hitting home that travel writing was usually written after travels themselves had already ended (Wyatt 2021).

Close relations to travel writing ranged from the unassuming forms of almanacs, recipe books, logs, diaries, and various court records to later public-facing texts. Studying the processing of travellers' texts can potentially capture the mobile lives of travellers who were both typical and untypical of travel writing studies – and the processes through which both their accounts and their presentations of themselves came into being. These texts also teach us different things, including the germs of ideas, the processing and composing of texts, and the divisions between what was intended for the wider public and what was not. For example, John Evelyn's 'diary', familiar to us as a record of his 'Grand Tour' and/or Civil War exile on the continent, was, according to Sean Silver, 'a hybrid document, an overlapping series of drafts assembled retrospectively from, on the one hand, notes scratched on almanacs, loose sheets of paper, and so forth, and, on the other, mnemonic aids not limited to public historical registers and fragments of material history themselves' (Silver 2015). Due to disciplinary divisions, we do not necessarily read Evelyn's texts as a travel account, even if his diary contained records of his travelling life, and was just as 'fashioned' as most travel writing of the period. Instead, his records have mainly been read for insights into his scientific and scholarly pursuits, and as evidence for his biography. I suggest that appreciating Evelyn's mobility and his self-fashioning in equal measures further illuminates his text, and not doing so results in missing a key opportunity. An example of appreciating mobility and self-fashioning is the commonplace book of John Sanderson that we read in the previous section regarding his embodiment, and his later printed account in *Purchas His Pilgrimes*.

In this section, I refer to the existence of visual images, maps, and appendices as testimonies to travellers' sensibilities, arguing that they helped fashion a traveller's self just as much as their textual records and travel accounts. The section will not only focus on travellers' material practices of writing but also on the ways in which their texts and records were connected to the practices of collecting and display, and on their visual representation. By examining the written and drawn mobile life of Peter Mundy (fl. 1597 – 1667), sometime Levant Company and EIC employee, I contend that mobile lives could be recorded and 'inscribed' visually and materially and become objects that were edited, maintained, and nurtured for an entire lifetime. By reading the manifold written and visual material records that a traveller like Mundy left behind through the lens of self- and life writing, I show how travellers' fashioning of the self could 'travel' between different textual and material forms in often surprising ways; during this process, the 'self' could also transform. The interplay of text and image was carefully contemplated: sometimes we discover more about Mundy's meanings and sometimes less, while occasionally the intended meanings seem clear. In addition, the manuscript's other visual aspects, together with their collection and assemblage, could present and 'fashion' the traveller's self, including their admirable intellectual and inquisitive qualities. Mundy is just one strikingly visual case study, of course, but his example can lead us to ask more questions about visual and material fashionings of the traveller, even in source materials that are plainer and not perhaps as obviously intentional in their representations of the traveller's self. Mundy can also act as an important reminder of how long the process of writing and editing travels could be, alongside authors such as Fynes Moryson, who famously took more than twenty years to publish his tractate on travels (Holmberg 2021a).

Embedded in diverse textual, visual, and material forms, which at first do not seem to contain constructions of the traveller's self, tracing travellers' lives across them allows scholars to dig deeper into the materiality and processes in which travel writings were presented and came into being, along with how they were intended to be read. Here the traveller becomes, in Sean Silver's words, 'a scholar or curator in the vanguard of the conservative, curatorial project of life- and history-writing,' a creator of their own mobile lives (Silver 2015, p. 339). Focusing attention on the materiality of Peter Mundy's texts and images provides us with new clues to the processes of how he constructed his travel writings, and as a result, on his fashioning and writing of himself, providing occasional glimpses into how this process changed during his long life.

In addition to offering clues to the traveller-writer's fashioning of themselves, materiality was often entangled with a traveller's specific aim regarding publication, showing signs of both ambition and intent towards social networks and relationships to other people and texts. It is useful to remember that many forms of publication beyond the printed folios and quartos were popular in the early modern period. Travellers could engage in manuscript publishing for a coterie audience, or they could reserve the manuscripts for only the eyes of family members and loved ones – or just themselves. Peter Mundy likely did not intend to publish in print. His manuscript is one of the richest, longest, and most fascinating texts about travels of this period, and is one of the most richly illustrated, which is an often under-explored feature to which we shall now turn.

Drawing a Mobile Life – Peter Mundy's Itinerarium Mundii and Its Images

The travels of Cornish merchant Peter Mundy (1597–1667) began when he was a young boy and an apprentice in 1611 and took him to many corners of the world, such as Istanbul, from Gdansk via the coast of Norway to Archangel, and several times to India in the service of the East India Company, trundling between the various English trading outposts. However, the impulse to record his many travels did not start immediately. His recording of the events of his life is thought to have started in the 1620s when he was returning to England from a posting in Istanbul as a Levant Company clerk.[28] Mundy's long life of travels was compiled into a manuscript entitled *Itinerarium Mundii* (in the Bodleian, MS Rawlinson A.315). The manuscript has 510 folio pages (255 leaves) and 117 images, most of which were drawn by Mundy himself, some on loose papers attached between folios. Mundy's earlier manuscript became lost when his father loaned it to a friend who did not return it; the first hundred pages of the existing manuscript in the Bodleian Library were thus copied by a scribe from another copy, while the rest is in Mundy's own hand (Palmer 2011).

On the title page, Mundy termed his work 'Itinerarium Mundii, that is a Memoriall', probably punning with his name and the multiple meanings of the word 'memoriall', which ranged from a work of memory to a rough version of merchant accounts. In fact, for an early modern merchant, the word 'memoriall' would have meant a rough version of an account or 'waste' book', from which accounts were transferred to a proper and neatly kept ledger. By naming his travel manuscript a 'memoriall', Mundy might have displayed humility in his literary endeavours while simultaneously connecting his text to the world of commerce and accounting from which he hailed. He could have also been aware of the resonances with 'memorials' and 'relaciones' in Spain, the observations and relations of reason of state, and the varied traditions of news writing on the continent (Mitchell 2022). Mundy later pasted small attached papers with additional subtitles in his frontispiece, where he recorded more 'journeys' and 'voyages' as they accumulated, including 'from 1611 to 1639; also unto some parts of Denmarck, Prussia, Polonia, and Moscovia or Russia, to the north side of the world, from 1639 to 1648; by Peter Mundy' and at the very end, an apologetic appendix, 'somwhatt concerning the former relationes, as allsoe matter of exercise and recreation after the reading of soe many tedious voyages and weary journies; Penrin, 4 Feb 1649' (fol. 208b).

---

[28] Mundy's writing ends later than his travels, and he continued to record local events and foreign news until 1667. For Mundy's biography, see Raiswell 2004.

At the beginning of his first 'relation' (fol. 2), Mundy added the distances or 'computation of miles' between places he had travelled at the start of his career as an apprentice in Spain and Gascony; in Istanbul, or' 'Constantinople', from Alexandretta and Constantinople, and from Constantinople to the mouth of the Black Sea, amounting to 17,394 miles at the time (fol. 2a/r). He continued this habit of adding up his life's miles at the end of each relation throughout the manuscript, including a 'petty passage' through England and some lengthy stays in Cornwall exploring local scenery.[29] At the end of his diverse relations in the Ottoman Empire was also an annotated map ('Turcici imperii imago', by Hondius), and Mundy continued to add annotated maps in between his relations where he traced his journeys over land and sea.

Prior to writing this surviving copy of the manuscript and during his travels, Mundy may have recorded his musings and impressions in note-books, which are now lost to us. Contemporary writers of apodemic texts often encouraged travellers to take note of 'everything' in order to not miss anything important.[30] From such a jumble of notes, travellers were supposed to later structure their experiences into suitable themes and topics – as scholars with their commonplace books and *loci communes* were already doing (Blair 2004). Mundy had intended to edit the text further and also expressed his wish to make an even cleaner copy of the whole manuscript and rewrite parts of it if he only had had more time.[31] Due to its voluminous nature, Mundy did probably not intend to print his *Itinerarium* as a book; rather, he more likely aimed to circulate it amongst very close friends – after all, an earlier version had already been lost due to careless handling and borrowing, and Mundy did probably not want to repeat this misfortune (Holmberg 2017).

In *Itinerarium Mundii,* some of Mundy's images can more easily be seen as portrayals of the travellers' selves than others, thus expanding our perception of drawings of people, events, and itineraries in travel writings. The more com-mon, or at least dominant, approach has been to consider images as either secondary to text or 'ethnographic images', which strive to construct knowledge about the foreign and exotic in their own way, with less focus on the constructor or 'assembler' of the images. According to Katherine Acheson, in this period, writing, painting, and drawing were becoming an 'index of subjectivity,

---

[29] Mundy's mileage 'from London to Constantinople by land by my computation amounteth unto 1838 miles.' Fol. 20a/r.

[30] Mundy's marginal notes and comments hint that he was a tireless editor of his own texts, intending to go through them at least once more with a proverbial red pen. For note-taking by travellers, see Bourguet 2010.

[31] Some folios have insertions that are dated later than the journeys. For the condition of the manuscript, see Richard C. Temple, 'Introduction', lvii-lxiii.

identified with gentlemanly virtue and Protestant modes of truth-telling'.[32] This promotion of art might have suited Peter Mundy's variety of purposes, even when they changed along the way, an aspect of the manuscript to which I will return below.

It is often difficult to determine when images in manuscript travel accounts were integrated into the texts, and whether they were drawn from sight or memory. Publishers of printed accounts usually used well-known and tried-and-tested maps, with very few woodcuts of engravings, as these added to the costs of printing. However, Mundy was quite informative about the many images in his *Itinerarium*, which helps us more easily interpret their meaning. In the separate preface (fols. 3 r-v), he tells about their construction; explains how he drew them (and hoped them to be better), and what he intended to do with them in the future, that is, replace them with better images, perhaps prepared by a professional illustrator. Mundy tells that the drawings ('Designes or Figures' ... 'were nott taken att Sight (Most of them) as they oughtt to have bin, butt long after, by apprehension off such things seene.' (fol. 3 r). He claims to 'have no skill in portaicture' and that he 'endeavoured to express the Most Meteriall[33] off the thinges mentioned.' These descriptions mean that his drawings were intended to be 'functional', and 'material', to assist people who had not travelled themselves to understand the substance of phenomena they had not seen with their own eyes.

How Mundy had learned to draw, we do not know; however, we can assume he was self-taught. Mundy had claimed to not be skilled in 'portraicture', which might be a common humility trope but may also tell the truth in that he probably lacked any formal training (Bermingham 2000; Levy 1974). He was neither an artisan, who would have had to learn the basics of penmanship for his trade, nor a gentleman or courtier, who might have dabbled in architecture or garden design; his schooling had mostly comprised basic education in the local school in Penryn. Additional skills in languages, arms and weapons accumulated during his apprenticeships and later postings abroad. Mundy gradually added more tools to his box of knowledge and experience throughout his life, reading well-received contemporary accounts of the places he had visited and displaying his reading in his retrospective writing of his travel relations. Additionally, he actively accumulated knowledge about foreign languages and customs, testified by several word lists, drawings, and trackings of the trade winds. He seems to have become more interested in plants, animals, and the natural

---

[32] Acheson here paraphrases Anne Berningham's study *Learning to Draw*. See Acheson 2016, p. 107.

[33] 'Material' here has meanings ranging from 'physical' substance to its 'wordly' and 'terrestrial' nature. See 'material, adj., n., and adv.' OED Online. Accessed 14 March 2023.

sciences the further and farther he travelled. His interest in foreign news and topical events continued until the very end of his life (Holmberg 2017). In his preface, all this 'life-long learning' was presented as a service to friends who might be interested in reading about foreign lands and as aiding his own 'remembrance', but may have also been intended as a family book and legacy, a theme which we will return to in the final, fourth section of this Element.

Alternatively, Mundy might have learned to scribble 'on the job', doodling when trade and commerce allowed, or later, when consulting maps and contemporary travel accounts. However, some of his own comments in both his writings and drawings hint at a more aspirational element. He stressed in his preface that he considered his literary and artistic exercises as a profitable way of spending his idle time and thought that writing should be 'reckoned among those recreationes Which are accompted honest and laudable (off Which sort are Musicke, painting, histories, civill Discours, etts)' – here he echoes both Aristotle and Castiglione, who strongly influenced contemporary ideas about drawing and painting (Mundy, vol. 1, p. 6).

Around the time Mundy put down his pens and quills, the Royal Society began to encourage all travellers to 'keepe exact diaries' and draw the coasts, islands, and ports they visited.[34] Coastal charting, mapping, and drawing of likenesses were also useful skills in British imperial endeavors; however, Mundy seems to have aligned more with the gentlemanly love of 'recreations' and creating a lasting memory of his own travel experiences.

Contemporary apodemic texts, for instance Thomas Palmer's *Instructions* (1606), had categorized painting among the 'instructions in knowledge fit for [gentlemen] travellers', which consisted of 'qualities, virtues and sciences.' These skills related to either travellers themselves or the country to which they travelled. Certain qualities, such as the necessary skill in languages, were prioritized over qualities 'for Ornation', which included drawing, music, dancing, and the carrying of arms, all of which were useful but not essential for every man.[35] Castiglione had recommended drawing to noblemen so that they

---

[34] 'To make plots and draughts of ye prospect of Considerable Coasts, Promontories, Islands and Ports, marking ye bearings and distances as neer as they can.' See *Directions for Seamen* by Lawrence Rooke (www.nma.gov.au/exhibitions/exploration_and_endeavour/take_ no_ones_word_for_it/transcript_directions_for_sea_men).

[35] Thomas Palmer, *Instructions* (1606), 38: ['practise in managing of Armes and weapons, skill in Musicke and daunsing and drawing the counterfeites of any thing']. A longer, more specific list of these 'ornaments' includes 'horsemanship, managing of all sorts of weapons, musicke, dancing, Poetrie, limming and portraiting, vaulting, running, and practising the fiue strengths of the arme.' The necessary sciences for travellers included 'insight in the grounds of Astronomie, Astrology, Cosmographie, Geographie, Hydrographie, Geometrie, Arithmeticke and Architecture'. These activities helped to make a journey successful, and aided travellers in storing knowledge in their memory.

could 'draw out Countries, Platforms, Rivers, Bridges, Castels, Holdes, Fortresses, and such other matters', that is, skills suited to their military duties (Levy 1974). For mariners and traders like Mundy, it would have been more useful to keep records of coastlines and itineraries and nothing else, but he did not stop at that.

Where did Mundy pick up this aspiration for visual collecting and display? Mundy might have consulted and appropriated the information in contemporary English drawing manuals, as he clearly did with the books of others on the Levant. Henry Peacham had published *The Art of Drawing with a Pen* in 1606, with a second edition, *The Gentleman's Exercise,* in 1612, which was accessible in London where Mundy lived between his voyages and until his move back to Cornwall. The latter edition advertised in its subtitle that it would instruct readers on how to draw various beasts and that it might be profitable to 'all young gentlemen and others' including 'tradesmen and artificers'. Peacham's later conduct manual, the *Compleat Gentleman* (1622), followed suit, intending to incite a love of art and its patronage in English gentlemen and to encourage homegrown talent in painting. Peacham wanted to reinstate drawing as a noble exercise and thus elevate it from a mechanical to a higher art form, and argue for its wide-ranging usefulness. The *Compleat Gentleman* presented art and 'painting' as necessary skills for all men who 'mean to follow the wars, or trauell into forreine countries' (Peacham 1622, pp. 108–9). It also recommended drawing to 'scholars' who had wearied themselves with books, could not go outside due to foul weather, or had no other way to profitably use their idle hours (Levy 1974). All these endeavours combine in Mundy's writing of his travels, which he saw, if not as a scholarly project, then at least a useful and pragmatic one.

The placement of images in *Itinerarium Mundii* was carefully planned: Mundy's drawings were 'drawne on loose papers' that were later 'pasted in', sometimes drawn directly on spaces left for them or inserted between folios and folded in half. He intended to replace some of the drawings later, and to add these 'in the void spaces left off purpose, and in the places off the other papers Now there Fastened' (Mundy 1907, p. 4). In a cut-out slip added on top of the text on the second page of his preface, Mundy also mentioned that he had 'inserted sundry mappes in seuerall places of this booke' (fol. 3 b/v).

There are several places in the manuscript where Mundy engages in visual displays of 'the travellers' self'. After the very first leaves of the manuscript, Mundy attached a printed cut-out world map by the Flemish mapmakers and engravers Jodocus Hondius (1563–1612) and Henry Hondius (drawn in 1630–31), which is dotted in a curious fashion (see Figure 1).[36]

---

[36] These were probably sold separately. For maps and their markings, see Dym and Lois 2021.

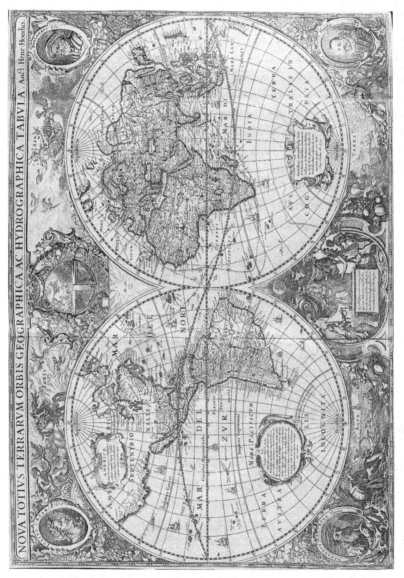

Figure 1 Detail from Mundy's *Itinerarium Mundii*, reproduced with permission from the Bodleian Libraries.

From Mundy's preface, probably composed in the 1630s after this map was printed, we learn that the markings traced both Mundy's actual journeys and those he had intended to make, preserving for posterity his alternative pasts and unrealized plans. The latter were 'traced with ciffres, Oes, or nulles' (fol. 3 b/v), including an ambitious crossing of the 'south sea' from Macao to Acapulco and continuing through Mexico that never took place. Likewise, the intended trip that Mundy had marked from Archangel to Moscow that would have ended his eventful journey via the coast of Norway to Russia was never realised. In this way, Mundy 'personalised' his Hondius map and made it into something between a memento of his own imagined and actualised itineraries and a diary list of places to visit, noting down both past adventures and events that never materialised. Regardless of whether his unrealized plans had a didactic element, Mundy's map of his life's travels shows that, in addition to his travels, he wanted to remember and preserve plans that never came into fruition. Mundy had wanted to go everywhere and see everything, but eventually his age caught up with him, and he ended his manuscript back home in Cornwall, keeping track of news of the world that he had already left behind, perhaps signifying to his readers that even if his own feet no longer travelled, his mind still did.

In addition to maps and drawings, the *Itinerarium Mundii* included a few cut-out print engravings that were either pasted in 'slots' reserved for them or on the verso sides of the folios.[37] Some of these images were attached to the verso side directly after the preface, table of contents, and index (fols. 2–8) and included three engravings: one of Francis Drake[38] (c. 1540–28 January 1596), one of Thomas Cavendish[39] (or Candyssh) (1560–1592), and one of a man of war below them, identified by the Bodleian cataloguers as a cut-out from Wenceslaus Hollar (1653) (fol. 8 b/v).

These images of the great 'Elizabethan sea-dogs' of the previous generation, together with the dotted maps of Mundy's own intended 'circumnavigations', helped to connect Mundy's own travels to the famous seafaring adventures and 'circumnavigations' of his countrymen, and the sciences, skills, and knowledge necessary for all travellers: cartography and navigation.[40] The engravings not only participated in the recording and 'memorializing' of Mundy's life in his *Itinerarium*, but I argue that they also helped him display himself as a great

---

[37] The other cut outs consist of city views (of Macao for example, fol. 135v.) and printed engravings of female dress.

[38] 'Franciscvs Draeck, Nobilissimus Eques Angliae Anno Aet. Sve 43.'

[39] 'Thomas Candyssh Nobilis Anglus Aeta Sva XXVIII'.

[40] Suzanna Ivanič has argued that 'the ways in which the writer of the travelogue adopts and adapts visual images reveals his association with various 'affinity groups' and thereby locates his identity at the intersection of a number of different groups.' See Ivanič 2015.

Figure 2 Detail from Mundy's *Itinerarium Mundii*, reproduced with permission from the Bodleian Libraries.[41]

traveller, following in the footsteps of Drake and Cavendish. The images helped to articulate his thoughts and served as a testimony of Mundy's character and achievements, curiosity, self-education, and intellectual aspirations in a collection of his own hard-earned travel knowledge (See Figure 2). Such aspirations continued

---

[41] For descriptions identifying these images and their sources as Hondius, Thomas le Leu, after Jo Rabel, and Hollar, see https://archives.bodleian.ox.ac.uk/repositories/2/archival_objects/248997

until the very end of the manuscript, where Mundy wrote down his observations about earth and stars, scientific inventions, and made a *volvelle* – a cousin of the astrolabe – out of paper.[42] As has already been mentioned above, several annotated maps by Hondius were attached between his relations and tracked his journeys between home and abroad throughout the manuscript.

Most of Mundy's own drawings in his *Itinerarium* can be categorized into four groups. The first group includes drawings of exotic animals that he had seen in South-East Asia, and included a shark (fol. 27 b/v), suckerfish (113 r), elephants carrying wood (158 v), 'strange sea snails' (113 v) and a dodo, which Mundy claims to have eaten (fol. 162 b/v).[43] The next group consists of impressive panoramic views and ceremonial processions that were attached in-between folios and could be folded out, including a procession of the Great Mogul Shah Jehan (1592–1666) from Brampor to Agra (attached between folios 68 v and 69 r and another between 69 v and 70 v). The third group included depictions of local men and women in their daily activities, dancing, worshipping, or, for example, eating with chopsticks (fol. 137 v). Mundy also started recording observations about winds and weather on his long sea-journeys to and from India (see fols. 100 r-v, 'From Suratt to England in the Roiall Mary'). The drawings were either fitted to the text at the time of making the manuscript copy, attached between the folio leaves as were the panoramas, or pasted to the verso side of folios as were the cut-out engravings from other sources. Mundy also started to include his own drawings, mostly of women's hats and clothing around fol. 130, which could be conceived as the fourth group of 'ethnographic images' of dress, thus following and adopting European-wide trends in costume books and *albae amicorum*, which were his likely generic models (Radway 2023). This type of drawing may have intended to connect Mundy's manuscript to the aspirational functions of the latter genre, which was utilized by young educational travellers to document not only their journeys but also social connections made during travels.[44] In fact, Mundy often also listed people he travelled or stayed with, and his employers and colleagues, all in a much more favourable way than John Sanderson (Holmberg 2021b).

The drawings by Mundy's own hand start after his relation about the Ottoman Empire, with images of Ottoman pastimes, festivals, and some gruesome

---

[42] For Mundy's scientific observations and largely inaccurate calculations, see Hunt 2018.

[43] Some of these include notes with addenda, where details of the creatures are added, along with the date of the addition. See for example *Itinerarium Mundii*, Fol. 113.v. Strange sea snails. Drawing and note from year 1649. Addendum.

[44] For such images, see Mundy's depictions of women of Sumatra and the Moluccas, and of Aceh. Fols 130r–130v.

executions.[45] These drawings served the function of visually documenting his own experiences, even if in retrospect, and are in direct dialogue with both his text and his readers. Mundy even accounts for his readers' potential sensitivities by announcing after a long description of various Ottoman tortures such as 'staking, gaunching, and 'drubbing, or beating on the feete' described on folio 6, that 'To divert your thoughts from those most cruell and torturing punishments I will digress to some of their pastimes and among those to the severall sorts of swingine . . . at their feast of Biram' (fol. 7 b/v).[46] Similar dialogical relationships with text and image exist in a small costume album, which Mundy had bought in Istanbul in 1618 ('PM 1618'), according to an inscription on its back. The album functioned as a visual compendium and appendix to his *Itinerarium Mundii*, with reminiscences and depictions of Ottoman social types, their customs, and their dress.

European and Ottoman costume books gained popularity from the late sixteenth century, along with various types of *albae amicorum*, a genre of friendship books or albums conceived in the context of elite sociability and travel. Susanna Ivanic has recently suggested that *albae amicorum* reflected the cosmopolitan identity of their 'constructor-owners,' something that Mundy possibly aspired to with both his Ottoman album and his manuscript relations (Ivanič 2015). Most of Mundy's own later costume images in his *Itinerarium Mundii* were depictions of female dress and headdresses, which were also common in *albae amicorum*, and he continued to record them until the end of his travel relations (Radway 2023).

Mundy's 'Ottoman' costume album had an interesting trajectory of hybrid co-creation, of which we do not know the full story.[47] Mundy had apparently bought a set of images painted by an unknown Ottoman bazaar artist that were pasted into a book in which he also recorded his own stories about the Ottoman capital and its inhabitants, probably after his return from the Levant in 1620. Mundy described the album and its function in the preface to his *Itinerarium Mundii*:

> For severall habits used at Constantinople, where most officers and Nationes are distinguished by their habits, I have a little booke, only of that particular, painted by the Turcks themselves in Anno 1618, although no great art therein, yet enough to satisfie concerning that Matter. (fol. 3)

---

[45] These are attached between folios 4 and 5 (festivities) and 5 and 6 (executions). Equally gruesome executions that Mundy had witnessed in Danzig/Gdansk were depicted on a flyleaf attached between folios 200 and 201.

[46] Mundy, *Itinerarium Mundii*, Fol. 7r.

[47] William Kynan-Wilson has pointed out that these kinds of albums were usually bought as mementoes, not as visual encyclopedias or as 'keys to understand the Ottomans.' See Kynan-Wilson 2017. For the album's construction and functions, see Collaço 2017.

Mundy considers his album as an addendum, filling a gap in his own manuscript which completes or at least adds to his collection of travels. Mundy also connects the images to his own recollections and experiences. Even if he did not mention this in his *Itinerarium*, the album also included texts in which Mundy both paraphrased existing accounts about Ottoman subjects – such as George Sandys' account that had already been published in 1615 – and corrected their descriptions and depictions. For example, he described Greek monks as 'the Coloieros [that] wear gownes of black of a homely stuffe with hoodes of the same and the haire at full length: as I remember they do at: Constantinople for here the turkish painter was deceived.' (fol. 54–55), indicating that he had eyewitnessed them differently from the Ottoman artist.

In his *Itinerarium*, Mundy expressed regrets about not starting to record his travels earlier, evidenced by the different versions and supplements to his first 'Relation', some of them written at the back of a cut-out map attached to the beginning.[48] He seems to have found the correct structure for his writing and the suitable placement for his images only later, as the writing of the manuscript advanced, adding and editing as he went along. Mundy's drawings multiply in the later relations, probably prompted by new expectations of the genre of travel writing, and exemplified by the engravings in the books he read and referenced in his *Itinerarium*. Earlier printed English travel accounts of the Ottoman Empire had not been very heavily illustrated due to their expense, but this changed towards the end of the seventeenth century (Brummett 2015). Only the skills of manuscript authors placed restrictions on illustration – in addition to the length and space allocated to the account.

Mundy had allegedly drawn his own images later, 'by apprehension off such things seene' during his own travels, and had clearly sought to learn more from other books in print. Mundy refers his readers to George Sandys' *An Account of a Journey* (1615) and Samuel Purchas' *Pilgrimage* (1613) as they covered topics more fully than Mundy, thus presenting himself as a modest, yet knowledgeable, collector-traveller-author who was useful to his readers, claiming to mainly focus on things he had seen with his own eyes. Influences by other categories of images are harder to trace, although his depictions of Mughal processions are similar enough to be based on Mughal models. It is also likely that Mundy consulted books on natural history when drawing fish or the scene of an elephant lifting and carrying firewood (fol. 158 b/v). As Mundy aimed to preserve knowledge by disseminating it to 'interested friends' and aiding his 'owne remembrance of things', he probably either modeled or at least checked his drawings against others on similar subjects.

---

[48] These leaves are attached to the beginning, before the first 'Relation', which re-starts from folio 1.

The value of a single picture of a dodo, elephant, or fish to 'writing a life' or partaking in Mundy's portrayal or 'fashioning' of himself may be questionable. It is easier to consider Mundy's 'fashioning' as a continuing and expanding practice throughout his long life via his various writings, pictures, and material possessions. To appreciate Mundy's life writing via its various material and visual means requires stepping back and thinking about the manuscript as an entity or 'collection' rather than a single item; it is like a visually rich collection that portrays a large sequence of Mundy's mobile life, displaying something that both he and his friends could return to time and time again. Mundy's impulse for keeping mementoes, recording, and collecting can be corroborated by the later, though somewhat sketchy, description by John Aubrey (1626–1697) in *Brief Lives*, where Mundy is portrayed as a 'merchant' and 'a great traveller' who 'wrote Memoires of all his journeys, a large folio, wherein he had draughts of their cities, habits, customs, etc. He had a great collection of natural rarities, coyness, prints, etc.' Aubrey had himself written a memorandum to 'Quaere for them', that is make inquiries about its existence.[49] We gain further evidence of Mundy's participation in the intellectual currents of his times by his own mentions of visiting both John Tradescant's 'rarities' and Sir Henry Moody's collections (fol. 108 r) in London between his arrival home from India in 1634 and his departure back, apparently the first eyewitness accounts of both.[50]

I have tried to illustrate that Mundy was not only a recorder but also a conscious 'collector' and curator of his own travels. His drawings, maps, and pasted prints tell a personal story of inquiry that involved collecting and memorializing, with the printed images and maps also indicating the kinds of associations Mundy wanted people to make and the global life of travels he wanted to portray. Observing or citing Mundy's images only in isolation or as examples of 'ethnographic' representation and knowledge production will make invisible this part of his authorship, hiding his self-writing below the surface. Mundy expressed that he considered his writings and his drawings as both a 'noble' exercise and a map of memory. He thus portrays not only the process of constructing knowledge about foreign lands but also the constructor's carefully fashioned scholarly and writerly *persona* (Algazi 2002). Just as the history of knowledge becomes enriched by considering material forms of artisan knowledge-making, and as life writing concerns the construction of communities and social networks, we might better understand an aspirational merchant by reading their account as aspiring or adapting to ideas that were

---

[49] *Brief Lives, chiefly of Contemporaries . . . by John Aubrey.* Clark ed. 1898 (vol. II. P. 90). Cited in Mundy 1914, p. lxxvi.

[50] For a comparable impulse to collect and preserve one's legacy by traveller and collector John Bargrave, see Bann 1994.

assumed to only belong to people above their station (Amelang 1998; Smith and Findlen 2013). Mundy's accounts in his *Itinerarium Mundii*, his costume album, and the diverse visual depictions of foreign life can fruitfully and significantly contribute to our understanding of the complexity of early modern travel writing and its closeness to life writing. By zooming out and considering the *Itinerarium Mundii* both as a carefully constructed material object and as a work of memory and visual recording of its author, we can see that it envisaged Mundy's lifelong practice of careful collecting, editing, and adding new layers and dimensions, becoming more than its constituent parts in the process. It was not just a testimony of travels but also an extension and a 'memoriall' of its maker. In the final section, we will delve deeper into autobiographical memory, and the impulse to 'recollect' and write the journeys after their accomplishment.

4 Afterlives of Travel: Memory Studies and Travel Memoirs

Travels performed a lot of cultural work, especially after the travels themselves had ended – making their afterlives deep, meaningful, and often contested. Travellers' writings were likewise often heavily shaped by events occurring after the mobile events themselves had ended. As one of the important building blocks of these 'afterlives', memory was considered subjective, fickle, and selective. This is especially true if the person doing the remembering was a traveller, because travellers were often suspected of embellishing their experiences and 'lying by authority' (Gallagher 2017; Hadfield 2017; Wood 2013). When the two phenomena, travel and memory, came together, their entanglement could both weaken and, in certain circumstances, strengthen the traveller's authority, provided they were approached the right way. A new flourishing of life writing around the middle of the seventeenth century also provided new forms where travel writing and remembering could take place.

Trying to hammer home the importance of memory, in his *Itinerary* (1617), Fynes Moryson instructed future travellers to write things down already during travels because otherwise, many things that the traveller had learned the hard way would vanish from their mind before they reached home. He instructed not to write down just anything but rather to seek to 'apply' the knowledge:

> And because the memory is weak, and those who write much, are many times like the Clerkes that carry their learning in their Booke, not in their braine, let him constantly obserue this, that whatsoeuer he sees or heares, he apply it to his vse, and by discourse (though forced) make it his owne. Thus Students of *Rhetoricke*, at first seeking matter for words, rather then words for matter, at last attaine an easie stile flowing like a still Riuer, and lay aside the affectation of words. Let nothing worth the knowledge passe his eyes or

eares, which he draweth not to his owne possession in this sort. In the meane time, though he trust not to his papers, yet for the weakenes of memory, let him carefully note all rare obseruations; for hee lesse offends that writes many toyes, then he that omits one serious thing, and after when his iudgement is more ripe, he shall distill Gold (as the Prouerbe is) out of this dung of Ennius. Let him write these notes each day, at morne and at euen in his Inne, within writing Tables carried about him, and after at leasure into a paper booke, that many yeers after he may looke ouer them at his pleasure. But great caution must be had, especially in places of danger, how he carry about him these papers, the subiect whereof, cannot but in many places be offensiue and perhaps dangerous, if once vpon suspition he chance to bee searched. Therefore as he sends his bookes and heauy things for carriage, halfe yeerely, either into his owne Countrey, or to some place in the way by which hee is to returne, there to be kept for him, so hee shall doe well to send these paper bookes therewith. And for abundant caution, lest any thing he notes by the way, should in any place vpon mischance preiudice him, he shall doe well to write such things in Ciphers and vnknowne caracters, being also ready to giue a fained interpretation of them to any Magistrate, if neede be.[51]

Individual lived experiences, including travel, were thought to fade from memory quickly, especially as people grew older. Consequently, it was important to define the valuable things to remember, learn them deeply, and determine the most effective note-taking techniques to apply during travels to ensure that no important thing faded from memory before returning home, or as was the worry of Moryson, got in the wrong hands (Bourgouet 2010).

Histories of knowledge and renewed interest in material texts have instilled curiosity among historians and literary scholars of travel about how travel writings came into being – before, during, and after travels, and also into how they continued to lead multiple, often unintended cultural afterlives.[52] A significant shaping power over texts, regardless of whether they published their texts in printed form or in manuscript, was the traveller's original intention to write about their travels. A person who travelled in order to eventually write about their travels could be seen in how they wrote; often, the framing of the account offers insight into what the traveller was trying to achieve (MacLean 2004b).

We have now arrived at the last section of this Element, where my readings are informed by research in Autobiography and early modern Memory Studies (Arnold and van der Walt 2018; Chedgzoy 2018; Wood 2014; Hodgkin 2020; Hodgkin and Radstone 2003; Wood 2013). It explores the complex retrospective composition processes of travel writing, which is further complicated by the travellers' relationship with time, the narrative construction of their texts, and

---

[51] Moryson, *An Itinerary* (1617): III. 12–13.

[52] For studies of mobility, where practices of recording have been centred see for example Corens 2018, Corens 2016; Williams 2019.

the in-built sense of immediacy of much travel writing. Instead of tracing travel writing for eyewitness reporting, it encourages us to approach them as diachronic memory texts in which the traveller heavily 'fashions' themselves in retrospect. This retrospective perspective offers scholars the opportunity to dig up much new evidence about traveller-authors' writing about their mobile lives, along with the processes of both the construction of the traveller's self and travel writing in general – at least when we expand our searches around these construction processes to include time before and after travels. Travel writings were socially constructed texts that endured numerous editorial interventions. Paying more attention to the 'traveller' in these texts helps place the authorial self in context, at least when we know when the traveller sat down and wrote their texts, and what kinds of resources they had at their disposal (Wyatt 2021).

Travellers often took a long time to write about their travels, employing the rich practices and cultural vocabularies of memory and commemoration available in early modern culture and widening the texts and resources they had at their disposal after their return. As Mary Fuller demonstrated, one of the main motivators of English early modern travel and colonial writings was 'remembering' and commemorating the heroic deeds of the English nation, along with the deeds of individual English explorers, seafarers, and colonisers – and encouraging others to follow their trails to faraway lands and newly founded colonies. Fuller reminded us, however, that English travellers often struggled to present their haphazard wanderings amidst frozen seas and strange fish as success stories reminiscent of their counterparts in Spain or New Spain (Fuller 2008; Hadfield 1998). The functions of travel and colonial writing in this period were deeply political: while often celebratory and commemorative, they were occasionally damning – especially when trying to put the blame on others for disastrous and reckless ventures or when seeking compensation for lost investments (Din-Kariuki 2020; Goldgar 2020). Sometimes, if things had gone wrong due to death, loss of money, mutiny, or such, clarifying your own version of events or at least trying to set the record straight became vital. Probably for this reason, Levant Company clerk John Sanderson composed an account of both his own actions and those of his closest colleagues and apprentice in the Levant to make sure that his version of the events was recorded (Brock 2021; Holmberg 2021). These more ambivalent writings often remained in manuscript and were available to a more restricted audience.

When trying to make an impact back home after travels had ended, subtle and diverse registers of self-writing and -fashioning came in handy, even when the surface motivation for writing concerned knowledge production and intelligence gathering. These histories of knowledge have been given far more attention than travellers' fashioning of themselves. It would be useful to combine these knowledge-building perspectives with other elements of the human experience: embodiment, emotions, and the many layers of retrospective processing of memory and recollection that gave these accounts shape and meaning alongside efforts at truth-telling and credibility-constructing. Much fashioning and representing of the self happened within these processes (Shapin 1994).

Some travel writings went through more complex processes of retrospective editing and reframing than others, which significantly shaped their presentation and later readings – as we can see in the example of the famous edited collections by Richard Hakluyt and Samuel Purchas. Both editors presented often heavily redacted and strategically structured travellers' accounts, detaching them from their original contexts of creation, and often organised them both periodically and geographically, with repetitions either accentuated or chopped off.[53] Unfortunately, we rarely have both manuscript and printed versions of these texts passed down to us; however, when we do, these operations are obvious, and the editors' voice quite audible (Carey and Jowitt 2012). These instances indicate who wielded the pen and power especially over printed travel writing collections, and how we should take these retrospective interventions by traveller-authors and their editors into account when reading these texts either for travel experience or memory. It is therefore also worth asking whose memory is shaping these texts, and how this might have also shaped our readings.

Looking at and interpreting travel writings through the combined lenses of life-writing, self-fashioning, and autobiographical memory will, I suggest, help maintain focus on who is doing the constructing and fashioning, who had the power to shape what was retold and recollected about travels and why. Remembering the shaping power of memory and its often hard-to-trace operations will lead scholars to ask questions from travel writing that should be just as complex and nuanced as those asked of contemporary autobiographical writings and memoirs – regarding credibility, retrospective embellishment, and a wide variety of fictions and fashioning of the self. For this endeavour to be productive, however, scholars of early modern travel writing must learn from the contributions of scholars of early modern autobiographical memory and life writing, who have already done much work in unravelling the psychological complexities of early modern writers – rather than either trying to reinvent the wheel or battle with the problems of 'Modernity' too much (Baggerman, Dekker, and Mascuch 2011). The early modern period had its own rich memory cultures, meanings, and practices that open new avenues to explore travel writing as a valuable form of life writing, alongside further records of mobility in texts in other, often overlapping genres. Participating in this line of

---

[53] For the Tudor travels, and their processes of later editing, see Matthew Dimmock's earlier Element in this series.

scholarship is crucial in helping us to follow travellers throughout their travels, from departures to returns, already before they started leading mobile lives, and most crucially, to understand how their mobility shaped the writing of their entire lives, how it mattered to them beyond the length of their travels. Following travellers through the changing sceneries of their mobility – not only in specific geographies, a common tendency in studies of travel writing – reveals often lifelong trajectories of continuous and perpetual mobility. In capturing these contexts, an auto/biographical and life history approach is vital (Corens 2018; Sau and Eissa-Barroso 2022).

The early modern period had rich cultural frameworks and vocabularies to discuss the workings and functions of memory: writers knew its fickleness and understood its physical and mental operations. Just as in later periods, when the early modern bodies and minds grew older, they likewise thought that memories of youth and childhood were likely to start fading. This forgetfulness was fought against with tips and tricks, memory palaces, notes, scribblings, and records, and ultimately by writing things down, due to the awareness of how unreliable memory could be.[54] In this, travel writing was no exception. Like other texts that were products of memory and experience, it too was created using vast cultural vocabularies and resources that the traveller could tap into later, most often after returning home. Even when writers stressed that they had seen the events and phenomena with their own eyes, their experience was still heavily mediated, refashioned, and reconstructed. Despite being based on earlier notes and drafts, travel accounts were usually retrospectively collected, often heavily utilising other travellers' materials. Consequently, travel accounts were strongly shaped by the powers of personal memory, contemporary practices of note-taking, and citation as well (Blair 2010, 2004; Bourguet 2010; Daston 2004). In the absence of many surviving notebooks by specific travellers, and when direct corroborating evidence is scarce, apodemic texts and subtle hints in published travel texts can reveal more about the practices of memory that shaped travel writing. These texts gave advice on how to draw maps of a new city from memory after a first visit, or on how to jot down notes based on eye-witnessing and conversations with local people. Others mentioned in passing how they trans-ferred their notes from one form to another during their journeys.[55] Other ephemeral evidence about the writing of mobile experiences can be garnered

---

[54] A memory palace is a mnemonic technique that was known and practiced by writers such as Fynes Moryson and William Lithgow. For memory palaces, see Carruthers 2008 (1990).

[55] See Thomas Palmer, *Instructions* (1606). Fynes Moryson mentioned that upon arrival to Jerusalem, even if unskilled in geography, he first drew a map of the city. See Moryson, *An Itinerary* (1617):I. 217–218. For note-taking see also III.12–13. Henry Timberlake mentioned in passing that he wrote things down in his quarters after a long day sight-seeing in Jerusalem. Timberlake, *A True and strange discourse of the trauailes of two English Pilgrimes* (1603):12.

from 'travel archives' or 'travel collections', of which fewer survive from the early modern period than later times, in which travellers kept objects, books, and documents commemorating their travels. We have already encountered such survivals by John Sanderson and Peter Mundy, and we should try to search for more, and if not in material form, then at least as 'hauntings' of textual references to objects, images, and texts that are now lost (Arnold and Walt 2018).

Retrospective recollection and construction not only shaped the content of travellers' writings; it opened them up to new political relevance. Travel accounts, like news texts, were deeply connected to geopolitical changes: they were also often shaped to fit the interests of changing patrons and potentates with diverse political stances and preferences, and their authors adapting networks of publishing and patronage. William Lithgow, a professional writer whose intention in travelling during a turbulent time was to subsequently write about the travels, spent a lifetime reshaping and editing his works for new audiences. In his *A Most Delectable and Trve Discourse* (1614), which he dedicated to the Earl of Somerset and his wife, Lithgow reminded his 'Courteous Peruser' that he had actually made 'double paines, of a two-fold Pilgrimage; first, in my personall prograce, to these famous places, and next a second peregrination of mind, in renewing the same in the Map of my owne Memory' (Lithgow 1614, sig. A3 v). Lithgow prepared new editions of his book with added details and themes that had been pared down in their first versions. In the process of embellishment, the narrative gained more texture and detail, often alongside anecdotes and added side notes. For example, to his 1632 edition of *A Totall Discourse of the Rare Adventures*, Lithgow added a scene where he challenged a Greek impostor in London, seeking to prove that the Greek had never been to Jerusalem as he had claimed. By writing this scene, he was probably catering for the interests of an audience that had recently encountered Greek refugees from the Ottoman Empire and were suspicious of them.[56]

The previous sections have illustrated that foreign long-distance travels were an important part of travellers' lives, equipping them with expertise, travel knowledge, and intelligence, which could be applied to gain both new occupations and credentials. The benefits of travel were recognised: travel provided experience and intelligence, which were lauded in contemporary political and apodemic texts. Additionally, travel had educational value, even if this issue was simultaneously hotly debated (Williamson 2016). No wonder travellers wanted to both commemorate these periods in writing and benefit from their travels in their future lives, or at least defend the expertise they had gained along the way against accusations that these were either suspect or useless altogether.

---

[56] For Lithgow's negative portrayals of Greeks, see Mitsi 2017, pp. 31–32; Bosworth 2006, pp. 44–45.

If a traveller was trying to secure a position or patronage with the help of their writing, it was vital to know whom to address and dedicate their accounts to in order to maximise benefit. However, the people involved often changed quickly due to dynastic and party-political turbulence. Making a living through writing in this period was still difficult, so travellers commonly tried to gain other kinds of perks and allotments, and to show already existing connections to gain new ones. A good example of this kind of practice is Henry Blount's *A Voyage into the Levant* (1636), where Blount combined the perspective of a courtier and thinker in the tradition of 'reason of state' with being a shrewd and witty observer of Ottoman lands, which often, though perhaps not always, owed to his own eyewitness experience (Din-Kariuki 2023). Blount carefully fashioned himself in his texts as an experienced, critical, and resourceful man, just the kind of man who would be useful to have around both at court and in the country. This effort shaped Blount's accounts, not just of how he presented the Ottoman lands but also himself wandering through them (Holmberg 2021c).

Sometimes travellers took a very long time to publish or write down their 'travels', making a strong case for the exploration of the workings of their memory. The thoughts of Moryson, who had travelled in the later years of the Elizabethan reign, finally emerged only in 1617. He first wrote a version of his treatise in Latin, then translated it to English. However, a large part of his treatise remained in manuscript and never reached print (Kew 1995; Parkinson 2012). We should heed not only the practices of recollection and record-keeping of a writer such as Moryson but also the retrospective processing, editing, and memorializing of travel accounts in general – both as a personal and sociable experience and as a fashioned and strategic creation of 'memory texts' and social and more private 'selves'. This could mean exploring travellers' texts in the context of their other writings, if available to us; their correspondence, or their intertextual links to accounts in existence, of which they borrowed either lightly or heavily, or looking at varied manuscript versions of their text, or even the editing processes of a single manuscript, if they show significant signs of this.[57] Remembering this retrospective construction when reading travel writing will help us better notice citationality, editorial interventions, and practices of early modern publication in both print and manuscript form, to the extent that we might wonder where the agency and authorship of the traveller and their fashioned 'self' is situated in all these interventions (Din-Kariuki 2023; Das 2016). We might also notice where the traveller's own emotional connections to events are so strong that they decided to commemorate the events in their texts not just to advance knowledge

---

[57] Moryson's fashioning of himself and his brother's memory resurfaces in several parts of the treatise. See Holmberg 2021a.

but also to keep their loved ones alive. For example, Fynes Moryson's treatment of his brother Henry's death during the brothers' travels in the Levant both warns about the dangers of early modern travel and highlights how, despite the painfulness of the memory of the event, Moryson still decided to write about it in several places of his great tome, many years after the events (Holmberg 2021a). These kinds of long-distance memories and commemorative practices may also be further explored by paying more attention to aging and nostalgia, and the resulting effects on travel authors' reminiscences of their youth, or when they became increasingly aware of their own mortality and advancing age, which some have defined as a 'gerontological' perspective. Noticing changes in interests, themes, and practices of recording, or just the increasing frailty of the author's handwriting can all provide clues to the effects of their ageing, including an increasing interest in the afterlife, sin, and redemption – although it must be said that the rise of spiritual autobiography in the middle of the seventeenth century also contributed to such interests (Chedgzoy 2018; Jarvis 2018).

In travel manuscripts, the retrospective practices of authorship – as of editing – were often more visible than in printed texts; even there however, the workings of recollection could be sometimes hard to detect. It is therefore illuminating when we can clearly see the author in action, editing, redacting, and rewriting their account, while commenting on their own practice as they go. One such early modern author, whose account was a forum for their mobility, spiritual ponderings, and efforts to pin down memories that were quickly fading, was Richard Norwood (1590–1675). Norwood is most famous for being the first surveyor and mapmaker of Bermuda, and the author of a spiritual autobiography, which dedicated a long stretch of its pages to Norwood's wayward mobility in his youth (Bendall 2022; Hodgkin 2016). For Norwood, travel brought back painful memories that he did not necessarily cherish. For him, mobility could even be conceived of as the bane of his existence or at least an obstacle in the way of his salvation; the interpretation depended on the type of literature in which the stories of travel happened to be embedded, and his happened to be embedded in a spiritual autobiography. According to Katherine Hodgkin, in early modern spiritual autobiographies, 'the focus on inner rather than outer life disrupts temporality and leads to wildly varying levels of detail in relation to the defining elements of modern selfhood' (Hodgkin 2017).

Norwood's spiritual autobiography '*Confessions*' has not been read so much as an account of mobility, but rather as an account of Norwood's struggles with faith. I argue that these two themes productively illuminate each other.[58]

---

[58] Richard Norwood, 'Confessions' (1639–40), 4105 – 003 PA 0307, Bermuda Archives. All following in-text references are to the folios in this manuscript. I have also written about these themes in a forthcoming article, to be published in the *Huntington Library Quarterly* in 2024.

In *Confessions*, Norwood deeply regretted his youthful wanderings around war-torn continental Europe and his 'pilgrimage' to Rome. Yet, he simultaneously seemed keen to write about his adventures and explain them as something he was forced into due to the lack of familial support for his choice of 'calling' for a mobile and seafaring life. Luckily for us, Norwood had adopted the Protestant ideals and practices of confessing his sins on paper. He saw writing and keeping his memories alive as a useful religious practice. In the process, he not only confessed his youthful sins but also noted down the many times providence and God had shown him mercy in his life and saved him from his inner demons. Norwood's text formed part of the seventeenth-century flourishing of spiritual autobiography, which was only one aspect of the growth and widening cultural importance of biographical and autobiographical writing in that century. This topic is vast and wide-ranging, and it is not possible to tackle it here at length. It included humble religious life writings and also biographies of scientists and noblemen, and ranged from the likes of John Aubrey to women's legacies to their children. It could be explained both by the greater availability and afford-ability of paper and the growth in printed exemplary texts that non-elite authors could creatively appropriate and use as templates (Pritchard 2005; Stewart 2018; Smyth 2010).

I am not claiming here that Norwood's *Confessions* was merely, or first and foremost, a travel account, or that it was even mostly about his travels. The manuscript was clearly an early example of a spiritual autobiography in which Norwood's accounts of mobility were nested and preserved, although also, regretfully, overlooked because other aspects of his text were more interesting to scholars. I argue here that reading Norwood for his 'mobility' and his practices of autobiographical memory provides a rich new avenue to explore his authorship, which also helps to show his spiritual life in a new light – as it was deeply shaped and structured by his mobility. In his manuscript, Norwood left an important record not only of his travels and his 'travails' in the valley of sin but also a testimony of how his memory and practice of 'recollection' worked in producing his account.

When approaching his fiftieth year, Norwood noticed that some important events and thoughts had started to 'grow out' of his memory.[59] By writing about things that had happened to him, he intended to keep these events in his mind and preserve them as lessons both for himself and possibly for posterity. However, some of this material was visceral and sensitive to modern eyes. For example, among his many sins of a sexual nature, Norwood confessed to having suffered from not only 'addictive' reading habits and theatre going but

---

[59] These first preface-pages as unnumbered. See also Craven and Hayward 1945.

also being unable to refrain from his 'major sin', masturbation, which he also called a 'stain' on his life. When writing his account of his life, Norwood mentions sources that help his memory: some 'catalogues' in which he had recorded both his experiences at the time of his conversion in Bermuda in 1617 and a list of sins and providences that had manifested in his life so far. He claimed these sources were '*a great helpe to my memory in many thinges*' when he composed the manuscript, writing on Saturday afternoons or when he happened to have time from his other duties – teaching, farming, and providing for his family that had recently emigrated to Bermuda after Laudian persecution of non-conformist Christians.[60] Norwood mentions having taken a year to write down his early life – the manuscript ended with events of 1620 or so, before he managed to introduce his marriage or his later years in Bermuda. However, he had, at least initially, intended to write down 'the whole course of his life past' and 'how the Lord had dealt with' him but when he had

> ... perceived that some things beganne to grow out of memory which I thought I should scarce ever have forgotten; and considering that as age came on forgetfulnes would more increase upon me, I determined then to sett them downe in Writing.[61]

Unlike many edited and printed accounts of travel, in the above passage, Norwood tells us his reasons for beginning to write and on what kind of notes he based his text, which is evidence of personal motivations that are often lacking in printed travel writings, and impulses that are also often taken for granted. The account combines the layers and levels of time: the time of writing, the time of later editing and redaction, and of course, the times of Norwood's experiences of both travel and spiritual woes. The account thus collects the layers and perspectives of a long life, and even beyond, in its retrospective editing and processing. Due to its personal nature, Norwood did not intend his manuscript to be public-facing; however, did he envisage that it would be read by other people at all? After all, most early modern spiritual autobiographies had this kind of didactic and memorialising function, and Norwood certainly was aware of them (Lynch 2012).

The text is entangled with early modern memory culture in several ways, namely in the suggested connection between the scripting of the self and family memory and legacy (Pollman 2017). Spiritual autobiographies were often intended as lessons and legacies to offspring, envisioned as being preserved and circulated in the same way as family books and Bibles (Walsham 2023).

---

[60] See Sarah Bendall, 'Norwood, Richard (1590–1675), Surveyor and Mathematician | Oxford Dictionary of National Biography'. Accessed 1 December 2022. https://doi.org/10.1093/ref: odnb/20365.

[61] Richard Norwood, 'Confessions' (1639–40), 4105 – 003 PA 0307, Bermuda Archives. Unnumbered preface. All following references will be to the pages in this manuscript.

However, Richard Norwood's will does not include a direct reference to *Confessions*, apart from a short passage in which he left 'the rest of his books and manuscripts' to his two sons, the most likely recipients of such texts.[62] Norwood's other books – both in print and manuscript – along with his assets, had been carefully divided between his three children, including his surveying equipment, his house, and his slaves – which Norwood did not set free. The books in the library of Norwood's school were scattered more widely, some finding their way either to his personal library or beyond, in Bermuda or unknown special collections from where it is impossible to trace them anymore (Lefroy 1981, pp. 58–9).

At the time of his death in 1675, Norwood was naturally no longer the wandering and wayward youth he had been reminiscing about in his *Confessions*, but a settled *pater familias*, probably more concerned about his assets and legacy than all the disappearing memories of his youth, which might explain why some parts of his confessions were redacted by smudging them with black ink. Some of these smudgings were possibly made by the author of the text; however, they could just as easily have been made later by an offspring who was trying to guard Norwood's legacy. Much of the material in the manuscript could have been incendiary to family, associates, and the high and mighty of Bermuda, creating problems for Norwood's family even beyond the grave. Norwood's concentration on his severe regrets about his sexual sins might have also been unsavoury to later readers. Our reading of Norwood's texts is affected by whether we think he censored it himself or if this was done by his son, who kept his literary legacy going, managing the reprinting of Norwood's tracts on navigation, mathematics, and geography. Rather than reading Norwood's changing psychological states from a text that was the product of a long period of experiencing, writing, and re-processing, we should take these different layers of time into account when reading him for embodiment, passions, nightmares, or his religious conversion(s).

Norwood's text was citational, residing, and embedded in the culture of both spirituality and mobility. Amidst discussions of personal faith and sin were some of the most precarious and wayward aspects of Norwood's mobile life. During the period that could be called Norwood's 'hyper mobile' years, falling roughly between 1605 and 1610/12, Norwood left an apprenticeship in the shop of a London fishmonger for an apprenticeship in coastal shipping that involved transporting sea coal and fish to Newcastle (17–19). A brief posting in the Navy was followed by a short stint as a mercenary in the Dutch Wars, creating a sense that Norwood was tossed around in the rough seas of his fate, rather than

---

[62] See The will of Richard Norwood 1674, PP 107/3, The Bermuda Archives.

following a plan made by either himself or by God – who, as Norwood seems to think, had a plan for him all along. Norwood was the son of an impoverished gentleman, a man who had lost his farm and had to take his young son away from grammar school after only two years (p. 14, 81). This short schooling was a great tragedy for Norwood, and a deep wound he could have tried to heal by independent study and learning throughout the course of his long life. Despite all the excitement, Norwood's precarious youth may have caused him to taint his mobility at the time when later writing about this period in his life during his relatively settled state in Bermuda. Even then, Norwood was still suffering from and contemplating his own spiritual unrest, and the manuscript does not provide him with a settled conclusion.

In *Confessions,* from the perspective of middle age, Norwood recorded his youthful worries about his future, his faith, and the lack of familial support for a mobile life of seafaring. These concerns may have served a dual purpose: a partial reasoning and retrospective explanation for his decision to travel to Rome after fighting in the Dutch Wars (pp. 29–30), where he pretended to be a pilgrim, or at least claimed to have dissimulated. Being a potentially wavering Protestant visiting Rome was a scandalous thing to admit and would have landed him in trouble in 1612, a time that was in the aftermath of the famous Catholic plots. An additional motivation may have been to warn his offspring about the dangers of travel and Catholicism that lurked around all innocent and wayward youths, and thus ensure that his own sons chose different paths to their father. As Norwood confessed, the severity of his decision to travel 'greived [him] exceedingly' so much so that

> ... beeing much perplexed in minde with objections on both sides, and in consideration of my forlorne condition and no longer able to contayne my selfe I went aside out of the way into the standing corne (beeing harvest time) and there wept aboundantly till I think I was something distracted (p. 30).

Norwood not only wept in the middle of a Flemish cornfield but also travelled by night, presumably to avoid being stared at or judged for his decisions. To be fair, travelling by night might have also been a safety measure, but it also served to emphasise Norwood's later regrets about his wanderings.

Norwood found himself in the middle of Flemish fields in 1609, a turbulent year in European history. A fragile peace had been declared that summer between Spain and the United Provinces, and hostilities had ended for a brief period after the armistice was signed in Antwerp on 9 April. A leaf of the manuscript presenting the events during the war had been ripped off at some stage, leaving a gap in the narrative between Norwood joining the army and ending up in the Flemish countryside, weakened by an unnamed illness and consequent 'fitt'. The time and culprit of this act of redaction is hard to identify, although it may coincide with the hand-smudged confessions about his sexual sins and being sexually harassed by a Catholic priest on his way to Rome, a long description of which was redacted, illegible or too unsavoury to the first editor of the manuscript.[63]

Honest confessions of youthful sins were encouraged by Protestants who were worried about the effects of their sins on their salvation. Norwood admitted to being driven by curiosity, lust, and an intense 'will to travel' since an early age, although simultaneously wary of forsaking the faith of his father. A young Protestant man wanting to travel to Rome in 1609 required him to be both resourceful and well-organized: Norwood needed to first obtain a letter of recommendation from a Papal *nuntio* in Brussels. Another problem concerned Norwood, that is, prior to obtaining the letter of recommendation, he needed to convince the English Jesuits at Leuven of his sincerity and willingness to renounce his old faith and embrace the doctrines of Catholicism (pp. 32–33).[64] This journey was far too complicated and arduous to make if only motivated by curiosity and chance. The complicated nature of the situation is possibly reflected in the vagueness, uncertainty, and protestations in the text itself, along with Norwood's admissions of being more and more tempted by Catholicism the longer he continued his stay in Italy. His account seems sufficiently vague about all the teachings and rituals he participated in to create suspicion that Norwood's dissimulated conversion might have been more genuine than he later admitted.

Norwood's actions had weighed heavily on his conscience, which hints at a more serious spiritual transformation during his stay: he claims to have suffered from frightful visions, nightmares, and sleep paralysis, 'the mare', which started plaguing him immediately after crossing the Alps with 'Thomas', a youth in pilgrim's garb he was travelling with (p. 36). Norwood's earlier mentioned catalogues of his sins and 'mercies' (i.e. providence) in his life may have also recorded these sufferings. Moreover, the bookish Norwood, who had earlier in the manuscript expressed a predilection for both frivolous books and plays, might have been influenced by the picaresque novels, tales of knights errant, and comical interludes he claims to have been enamoured with at the time (pp. 21–22). Many close escapes were recorded, including being frozen in the Alps. Norwood also wrote about encountering dead bodies, prostitutes, murderous banditti, and wayward and robbing mercenaries on the way, which

---

[63] These redactions occur between pages 22 and 25 [ripped off], and on page 38 [Catholic priest]. There are smudges on several pages, which describe Norwood's sexual sins.

[64] For the Catholics of Leuven, see Whitehead 2016, p. 116. I would like to thank Dr. Liesbeth Corens for this reference.

all could create some suspicion in his reader, even if it was all still within the remit of what was possible. Early modern travel *was,* after all, a dangerous exercise, especially so if one travelled alone across a war-torn continent. Both memory texts and contemporary travel accounts were suspected of embellishments (Pfannebecker 2017). However, Norwood's presence in Rome in late 1609 is confirmed by both his own text and the pilgrim book of the English college, which records Norwood's arrival just before Christmas on 15 December.[65] Norwood wrote that he had first spent three nights at the 'hospital for that purpose', probably the famous *SS Trinità dei Pellegrini*, where he scraped the signature of the chancellery permitting him to stay some extra nights, and that: 'After this I was entertayned into the English Colledge there, for a month as I remember, where I was like to haue bene entertayned altogether but the Lord in his good providence had ordayned better for me' (Norwood 1639–40, pp. 33–4).

Norwood claims to have stayed at the college for longer than indicated in the pilgrim book of the college; although, the latter recording of eight days was likely a default, with poor pilgrims customarily staying longer and receiving alms, shoes, and sustenance.[66] Norwood confesses to engaging in Catholic practices, including praying with rosaries and making signs of the cross, even to the point of having planned a pilgrimage to Jerusalem and a trip to Sicily, of which he had read about in the Aeneid. He hints that he might have stayed for longer or for good, had not providence interfered. Norwood's account of his return to England gives testimony to his wavering views about religion and his family's efforts at 'unprogramming' Norwood from whatever he had become to return to be a pious Protestant youth, hinting that the path might have been rockier than he first admitted (pp. 47–48).

Remembering all these wavering wanderings of his youth was a spiritual duty for Norwood and an active form of penance for his many sins. From *Confessions,* we can read that Norwood blamed his curiosity for books and plays for further stoking the flames of sin, even influencing the course of his mobility. However, this curiosity was not the whole story; rather, precarity and lack of familial support had also contributed to his 'travails'. Somewhat frustratingly, the *Confessions* hops over most of Norwood's professional and family life from 1620 onwards, omitting his career as a teacher of mathematics, the creation of his family, and his return to

---

[65] The Pilgrim Book of the English College is being edited by Stefano Villani and Edward Chaney. I want to thank them both for sharing their transcriptions of Norwood's visit with me, indicating that Norwood stayed in the College for eight days, as was common for poor pilgrims, and not 30 days as he claimed in his 'Confessions': 'Die 15 December exceptus est in hospitium Rich Norwoode Hartfordiensis mansitque per dies per dies 8'.

[66] I want to thank Dr Maurice Whitehead for this information.

Bermuda. Instead, it focuses on the most mobile years of Norwood's life, admittedly the most sinful and transformative in the long narrative of his life. However, Norwood's later paper trails in the colonial records of Bermuda, his will, and his probate show that he did indeed lead a rich, relatively settled, and comfortable life later on when he did not have to uproot himself anymore.[67]

All these aspects, which suspend Norwood in a variety of timelines, remind us that *Confessions* was a 'memory text' to the core, even if the explicit contemplation of the functioning of Norwood's memory occurred in only a few instances: firstly at the beginning, when contemplating his vanishing memories of his life as a reason to write things down, and secondly, when describing his fear of God at the time of his conversion in Bermuda. In the first instance, Norwood was afraid of his fading memory, and in the second, he was afraid to write down his thoughts about his fear of God because he believed that writing them would further strengthen them when they were still 'fresher in his memory.' Norwood writes about this time:

> And I thinke I had written these thinges many yeares agone whilst they were fresher in memory, had I not observed this corruption, so to corrupt and poison my thoughtes and meditations of this kind, that I feared in setting them downe, I should expresse more winde and vanity, then truth and sobriety. (p. 149)

Implicitly, the *Confessions* showed in a variety of ways that the author was writing with hindsight. Its pages showed that Norwood had accrued additional knowledge and experience and had sufficient time and opportunity to put things into perspective, to contemplate his sins, choices, and aspirations in the context of salvation, providence, and often strained family dynamics, which were all shaped by the great narrative of Norwood's mobility, his search for a calling and peace (Capp 2019, 2018). First and foremost, a spiritual autobiography such as *Confessions* functioned as an aid to contemplation, repentance, and continuous re-reading. Luckily for us, as a by-product, *Confessions* preserved the memory of Norwood's precarious and perpetual mobility, which had made his rescue imperative for God.

5 Conclusion

A key moment in early modern travel writing, where the traveller constructs their 'self', includes the expression of gratitude to hospitable hosts: for offering food, lending money, sometimes curing illness, and providing support far away from home. Fynes Moryson, for instance, writing about his travels in the Levant

---

[67] See Eva Johanna Holmberg, 'An Unmoored life: Mobility, Reading, and Life-Writing in Richard Norwood's (1590–1675) *Confessions*', forthcoming in Huntington Library Quarterly in 2024.

in 1596–1597, decided to single out Levant Company factor George Dorrington
as the savior of his life. Dorrington had taken care of Moryson in Aleppo and
Iskenderun when he had suffered from a grave illness and grief caused by the
loss of his brother, and also provided Moryson with significant amounts of
money. He writes:

> Yea, when after my brother's death my selfe fell dangerously sicke, and was
> forced to goe from those parts before I could recouer my health, so as all men
> doubted of my returne into England, yet he [Dorrington] lent me a farre
> greater summe vpon my bare word, which howsoeuer I duly repayed after my
> comming into England, yet I confesse, that I cannot sufficiently acknowledge
> his loue to mee, and his noble consideration of poore and afflicted strangers.
> (Moryson 1617, I: 245)

In such performances of gratitude, ambassadors, factors, captains, and caravan conductors were the usual recipients of profuse thankfulness, either by
name if English or anonymously if they were foreigners and not famous or
likely to read the finished text. Helping an ailing traveller with no guarantee of
ever getting their money back was a powerful testimony of the generous
character of Dorrington. As Moryson explained further, Dorrington had also
recommended Moryson to investigate whether the sea-air would cure him,
contributing to his ultimate, even if incomplete, recovery. Moryson's grief-
stricken 'sicknesse' had been 'so vehement and so long, that all men doubted
[he] would neuer recouer':

> Yet when divers times I began to recover, and presently by the heate of the
> clime, and ill aire of the place, had been cast downe againe, I resolved to
> follow their counsell, who persuaded me to trie if the aire of the sea would
> strengthen me. Therefore my deare friend Master George Dorington having
> sent me one hundred zechines for my expences, the great summes of money
> which I had being all spent, by the accidents of my brothers death, and my
> sicknesse (the particulars of which expence I omit, because in this griefe and
> weakenesse I had no minde to note them, onely for a taste remembring, that
> I paid a piastro each day to a poore man, who continually cooled my heate
> with a fan (Moryson, *Itinerary* (1617), I: 251).

As I have argued elsewhere, Moryson decided to commemorate his own illness
and loss while simultaneously using his own experience to warn future travellers of a similar fate. In his didactic gestures, his own grief and illness were
effective examples of the ways emotions and the body were thought to be
intimately connected at the time. This horrifying experience was repeatedly
mentioned and dissected for both practical budgeting and health advice
throughout his *Itinerary* (1617). In these passages of his monumental treatise
on travel, Moryson not only created a lasting epitaph for his brother and his sad

fate but also relied heavily on his own visceral, embodied experiences of travelling (Holmberg 2021a).

This Element sets out with the claim that we should all be reading early modern travel writing for these kinds of mobile lives and bitter experiences contained in them; that is, equipped with the critical lenses provided by auto-biographical and life writing studies. The benefits of this would be multiple and enriching, not only for studies of travel writing but for early modern mobility in general, as I promised at the outset. Now that the Element is about to conclude, I can recognize some humility, caveats, and self-critical thoughts rising to the surface, partly for personal reasons – this project and ideas already started to germinate some years ago, while in the happy haze of writing the research proposal – and partly due to the rigorous processes of academic publishing and peer review, which always deliver authors ample amounts of humility.[68]

There is an autobiographical reasoning behind this Element as well, but the idea to put two vibrant fields of study into dialogue and look for how travel and life writing were entangled in this period was also something that arose from the sources themselves. Life circumstances might have also been an influence: I became more and more interested in the process of aging and nostalgia, as my own years seem to pass me by with increasing speed. I was writing about something else entirely when I came across some passages in Peter Mundy's *Itinerarium Mundii*, where after many years of travels Mundy was saying his goodbyes to London and going on solitary walks there before settling in his native Cornwall, certain that he would never return. His words struck me at the time. I was also about to leave London, sad and uncertain of my return, and almost by instinct, I was starting to turn my gaze from what was familiar to me, the traveller's gaze towards the foreign, to travellers' inner worlds. Relevance and importance can sometimes be found in these kinds of small, at first seemingly irrelevant yet emotional stories that had personal meaning to their author. Scholarship on such stories might not always win the big grants, but they still mattered to early modern people, and therefore should matter to us as well.[69]

It has been a conviction of mine that in order to investigate early modern lives and cultures more fully, we need to pay more attention to mobility and travel writing, and give it the same nuanced attention as any other practice or rich and multilayered source that documents it. Only in this way can we grasp the richness, ambiguity, and fullness of early modern mobile lives. Maybe we

---

[68] It goes almost without saying that this author is thankful for the two reviewers and her numerous friends, who took the time to read these words before they reach print.

[69] In this case they did even that, generously, and I would like to thank both the *Research Council of Finland* (artist formerly known as Academy of Finland) and, *The Finnish Cultural Foundation* for giving me a grant to write this small book.

also need to be more honest about what drives us to certain topics: having led an itinerant academic life might have led me to ask these questions or to study travel and mobility in the first place. That said, there are caveats to what I was trying to do here, and I wish others will carry the baton better than me – I wish this was a story less white and less male, and of less privilege. Some of my case studies might probably protest now if they came to life like Natalie Zemon Davis (1928–2023) famously brought her three women to life, and say that they were not privileged at all and that they did not 'get by with a little help from their friends' as the song goes (Davis 1995). The reasons behind analysing the texts of John Sanderson, Peter Mundy, and Richard Norwood are many, including my interest in merchants and mariners – a group that was in the early modern period very largely the domain of men – but I studied them also because something in their life and writing spoke to me: their challenges in their mobile work and community, their often protean presentations of themselves, which were shaped by their pride, humility, and self-pity alike, as well as their wish to record things, mostly for themselves and their friends, to keep their memories alive. Even if my case studies here were centered on men, many beacons of early modern life writing studies have been nuanced studies of women's writing and authorship, and I hope that by employing some of their insights here – when interpreting the complexity of illness narratives, the visuality and materiality of travel writing, and the many layers of memory – I have helped illuminate aspects of my three mobile life writers in new ways, and that these in turn would inspire studies of other travellers less privileged than mine, and of written mobile lives both before and after my own period of investigation. Luckily, I know such studies are already in preparation.

Like many authors at the beginning of a journey, I was certain of the relevance, importance, and even novelty of this line of inquiry. Now, at its conclusion, I want to acknowledge this relevance but also be humble about where this study sits. I want to make sure I duly recognize the scholars (quite a few of them friends) who have contributed to it. (This conclusion may, like the early modern genres I have been investigating, overlap with and share elements from 'acknowledgements' that are usually placed at the start of books.) My friends in this field have been an inspiration, as well as important critical allies in investigating the ways in which the writing of lives and travels were entangled in this period. These include Mark Williams, Nandini Das, Jyotsna Singh, Natalia Din-Kariuki, Kate Hodgkin, Samuli Kaislaniemi, Josephine Hoegaerts, Soile Ylivuori, Liesbeth Corens, John Gallagher, Richard Ansell, Richard Blakemore, Sarah Goldsmith, Tim Reinke-Williams, Josephine Hoegaerts, Rosi Carr, Charmian Mansell, Gabor Gelleri, Rachel Willie, Claire Jowitt, Mat Dimmock, Guido van Meersbergen, and Lubaaba al-Azami. All of them helped either by reading some of these pages, commenting on some papers, or inspiring me with their scholarship over the years. I also want to acknowledge the enormous help of my writing buddies Joanne Paul and Nicola Clark, as well as Kirsty Rolfe and Sara Norja, with whom our journey of editing Richard Norwood's *Confessions* is still underway. My first book was dedicated to my family, the second to my partner and my bunny, so it feels right to dedicate this one to all my friends. You know who you are, but I'd like to mention one in particular. This small Element is dedicated to you, Saara Kalajoki, with love.

References

Primary Sources:

Biddulph, William. 1609. *The Travels of certaine Englishmen*. London.

Clark, Andrew (ed.). 1898. *Brief Lives, Chiefly of Contemporaries ... by John Aubrey*. Oxford: Clarendon Press. (vol. II. P. 90).

Colley, Linda. 2007. *The Ordeal of Elizabeth Marsh. A Woman in World History*. London: Harper Collins.

Coryate, Thomas. 1611.
  Thomas Coriate Traueller for the English Vvits: Greeting from the Court of the Great Mogul, Resident at the Towne of Asmere, in Easterne India. London.

Fanshawe, Lady Anne. 1651–1707. *Mrs Fanshawes Booke of Receipts of Physickes, Salves, Waters, Cordialls, Preserves and Cookery*. Wellcome Library MS 7113.

Florio, John. 1611. *A Vvorlde of Wordes, or Most Copious, and Exact Dictionarie in Italian and English, Collected by Iohn Florio*. London.

Lefroy, John Henry. (ed.), 1981. *Memorials of the Discovery and Early Settlement of the Bermudas or Somers Islands 1511–1687: Compiled from the Colonial Records and Other Original Sources*. Vol. II, 1650–1687. Hamilton: The Bermuda Historical Society, The Bermuda National Trust.

Lithgow, William. 1614. *A Most Delectable and Trve Discourse*. London.
  1632. *Totall Discourse of the Rare Adventures*. London.

Moryson, Fynes. 1617. *Fynes Moryson's Itinerary*. London.

Mundy, Peter. 1907. *Itinerarium Mundii*. MS: Bodleian Rawlinson MS Add. 315. Cambridge. Printed for the Hakluyt Society.

Temple, Sir Richard Carnac and Lavinia Mary Anstey (eds). 1907–36. *The Travels of Peter Mundy in Europe and Asia, 1608–1667*. In 6 vols., London: Hakluyt Society. [All references are to this edition, parenthetically, to volumes 1, 5, and 6.]

Norwood, Richard. 1674. 'The will of Richard Norwood', PP 107/3, The Bermuda Archives.
  1639–40. 'Confessions'. 4105 – 003 PA 0307, Bermuda Archives.

Peacham, Henry. 1622. *Compleat Gentleman*. London.

Palmer, Thomas. 1606. *An Essay*. London.

Sanderson, John. 1931. *The Travels of John Sanderson in the Levant 1584–1602*. 2nd Serie; No. 67. London: Hakluyt Society.

Terry, Edward. 1655. *A Voyage to East India*. London.

Secondary Sources

Acheson, Katherine O. 2016. *Visual Rhetoric and Early Modern English Literature*. London: Routledge.

Agnew, Vanessa. 2012. 'Hearing Things: Music and Sounds the Traveller Heard and Didn't Hear on the Grand Tour', *Cultural Studies Review*, 18: 3: 67–84.

Algazi, Gadi. 2002. 'Food for Thought: Hieronymus Wolf Grapples with the Scholarly Habits', in *Egodocuments and History: Autobiographical Writing in Its Social Context since the Middle Ages*, ed. Rudolf Dekker. Publicaties van de Faculteit der Historische en Kunstwetenschappen Maatschappijgeschiedenis 21–44.

Ambrose, Laura Williamson. 2013. 'Travel in Time: Local Travel Writing and Seventeenth-Century English Almanacs', *Journal of Medieval and Early Modern Studies*, 43:2: 419–43.

Amelang, James S. 1998. *The Flight of Icarus: Artisan Autobiography in Early Modern Europe*. Stanford: Stanford University Press.

Andy Wood. 2014. The Memory of the People. Custom and Popular Senses of the Past in Early Modern England (Cambridge: Cambridge University Press).

Ansell, Richard. 2015. 'Educational Travel in Protestant Families from Post-Restoration Ireland', *The Historical Journal*, 58:4: 931–58.

Arnold, Lee and Thomas van der Walt. 2018. 'Collecting and Memory: A Study of Travel Archives', *Journeys*, 19:1: 52–66.

Baggerman, Arianne, Rudolf Dekker, and Michael Mascuch (eds.). 2011. *Controlling Time and Shaping the Self: Developments in Autobiographical Writing since the Sixteenth Century*. Leiden: Brill.

Ballantyne, Tony and Antoinette Burton. 2005. *Bodies in Contact: Rethinking Colonial Encounters in World History*. Durham, NC: Duke University Press Books.

Stephen Bann. 1994. *Under the Sign: John Bargrave as Collector, Traveler, and Witness*. Ann Arbor: Michigan University Press.

Beal, Peter. 1993. 'Notions in a Garrison: The Seventeenth-Century Commonplace Book', in *New Ways of Looking at Old Texts: Papers of the Renaissance English Text Society, 1985–1991*, ed. William Speed Hill. Binghampton: Renaissance English Text Society.

Beebe, Kathryne. 2014. *Pilgrim and Preacher: The Audiences and Observant Spirituality of Friar Felix Fabri (1437/8–1502)*. Oxford: Oxford University Press.

Bendall, Sarah. 2022. 'Norwood, Richard (1590–1675), Surveyor and Mathematician | Oxford Dictionary of National Biography'. Accessed 1 December 2022. https://doi.org/10.1093/ref:odnb/20365.

Bermingham, Ann. 2000. *Learning to Draw: Studies in the Cultural History of a Polite and Useful Art*. New Haven: Yale University Press.

Blaak, Jeroen. 2002. 'Autobiographical Reading and Writing: The Diary of David Beck (1624)', in *Egodocuments and History: Autobiographical Writing in its Social Context since the Middle Ages*, ed. Rudolf Dekker. Verloren: Hilversum, 61–87.

Blair, Ann. 2004. 'Note Taking as an Art of Transmission', *Critical Inquiry*, 31:1: 85–107.

2010. 'The Rise of Note-Taking in Early Modern Europe', *Intellectual History Review*, 20:3: 303–16.

Boddice, Rob. 2023. *Knowing Pain: A History of Sensation, Emotion, and Experience*. Medford: Polity Press.

Bosworth, Clifford Edmund. 2006. *An Intrepid Scot: William Lithgow of Lanark's Travels in the Ottoman Lands, North Africa and Central Europe, 1609-21*. Aldershot: Ashgate.

Bourguet, Marie-Noëlle. 2010. 'A Portable World: The Notebooks of European Travellers (Eighteenth to Nineteenth Centuries)', *Intellectual History Review*, 20:377–400, https://doi.org/10.1080/17496977.2010.492617.

Bourke, Joanna. 2017. *The Story of Pain: From Prayer to Painkillers*. Oxford: Oxford University Press.

Brock, Aske Laursen. 2021. '"Blackened and Whispered Away My Reputation": Fashioning a Reputation in the Late-Seventeenth-Century Levant Company', in *Trading Companies and Travel Knowledge in the Early Modern World*, eds. Aske Laursen Brock, Guido van Meersbergen, and Edmond Smith, Hakluyt Society Studies in the History of Travel; Vol. 1. London: Routledge.

Broomhall, Susan. 2016. 'Tears on Silk: Cross-Cultural Emotional Performances among Japanese-Born Christians in Seventeenth-Century Batavia', *Pakistan Journal of Historical Studies*, 1:1: 18–42.

Brummett, Palmira Johnson. 2015. *Mapping the Ottomans: Sovereignty, Territory, and Identity in the Early Modern Mediterranean*. Cambridge: Cambridge University Press.

Burke, Peter. 1992. *The Fabrication of Louis XIV*. Yale: Yale University Press.

Canning, Kathleen. 1994. 'Feminist History after the Linguistic Turn: Historicizing Discourse and Experience', *Signs: Journal of Women in Culture and Society*, 19:2: 368–404.

Capp, Bernard. 2019. 'Conversion, Conscience and Family Conflict in Early Modern England', in *Childhood, Youth and Religious Minorities in Early Modern Europe*, eds. Tali Berner and Lucy Underwood. Cham: Palgrave Macmillan, 319–40.

2018. *The Ties That Bind: Siblings, Family, and Society in Early Modern England*. Oxford: Oxford University Press.

Carey, Daniel. 2009. 'Hakluyt's Instructions: The Principal Navigations and Sixteenth-Century Travel Advice', *Studies in Travel Writing*, 13:2: 167–85.

Carey, Daniel and Claire Jowitt (eds.). 2012. *Richard Hakluyt and Travel Writing in Early Modern Europe*. Hakluyt Society Extra Series 47. Aldershot: Asghate.

Carruthers, Mary. 2008 (1990). *The Book of Memory: A Study of Memory in Medieval Culture*. Cambridge: Cambridge University Press.

Cavallo, Sandra and Tessa Storey. 2017. *Conserving Health in Early Modern Culture: Bodies and Environments in Italy and England*. Oxford: Oxford University Press.

Chaney, Edward and Timothy Wilks. 2014. *The Jacobean Grand Tour: Early Stuart Travellers in Europe*. London: I.B. Tauris.

Chedgzoy, Kate Elspeth Graham, and Ramona Wray. 2018. 'Researching Memory in Early Modern Studies', *Memory Studies*, 11:1: 5–20.

Coleman, Patrick, and Jayne Lewis, and Jill Kowalik (eds.). 2000. *Representations of the Self from the Renaissance to Romanticism*. Cambridge: Cambridge University Press.

Collaço, Gwendolyn. 2017. 'Dressing a City's Demeanour: Ottoman Costume Albums and the Portrayal of Urban Identity in the Early Seventeenth Century', *Textile History*, 48:2: 248–67.

Cooke, Simon. 2016. 'Inner Journeys: Travel Writing as Life Writing', in *Routledge Companion to Travel Writing*, ed. Carl Thompson. London: Routledge, 15–24.

Corens, Liesbeth, and Kate Peters, and Alexandra Walsham (eds.). 2016. *The Social History of the Archive: Record-Keeping in Early Modern Europe*, Past and Present Supplements, supplement 11. Oxford: Oxford University Press.

Corens, Liesbeth. 2016. 'Dislocation and Record-Keeping: The Counter Archives of the Catholic Diaspora', *Past & Present*, 230:suppl. 11: 269–87.

2018. *Confessional Mobility and English Catholics in Counter-Reformation Europe*. Oxford: Oxford University Press.

2022. 'Seasonable Coexistence: Temporality, Health Care and Confessional Relations in Spa, C .1648–1740'. *Past & Present*, 256: 1: 129–64.

Craven, Wesley Frank, and Walter Brownell Hayward (eds.). 1945. *The Journal of Richard Norwood, Surveyor of Bermuda*. New York: Published for the Bermuda Historical Monuments Trust by Scholars' Facsimiles & Reprints, 3.

Das, Nandini. 2016. 'Encounter as Process: England and Japan in the Late Sixteenth Century.'. *Renaissance Quarterly*, 69:: 1343–68.

2023. *Courting India: England, Mughal India and the Origins of Empire.* London: Bloomsbury.

Daston, Lorraine. 2004. 'Taking Note(s)', *Isis*, 95: 3: 443–48.

Davies, Surekha, and Neil L. Whitehead. 2012. 'From Maps to Mummy-Curses: Rethinking Encounters, Ethnography and Ethnology', *History and Anthropology*, 232: 173–82.

Davis, Lloyd. 2002. 'Cultural Encounters and Self Encounters in Early Modern English Travel Autobiographies', *Parergon*, 19:2: 151–67.

Davis, Natalie Zemon. 1986. 'Boundaries and the Sense of Self in Sixteenth-Century France', in *Reconstructing Individualism: Autonomy, Individuality, and the Self in Western Thought*, eds. Thomas C. Heller, Morton Sosna, and David E. Wellbery. Stanford: Stanford University Press, 53–63.

Davis, Natalie Zemon. 1988. 'Fame and Secrecy: Leon Modena's Life as an Early Modern Autobiography', *History & Theory*, 27:4: 103–18.

Davis, Natalie Zemon Davis. 2006. *Trickster Travels. A Sixteenth-Century Muslim Between Worlds.* New York: Hill and Wang, A Division of Farrar, Straus and Giroux.

1995. *Women on the Margins: Three Seventeenth-Century Lives.* Cambridge, MA: Harvard University Press.

Dawson, Mark S. 2000. 'Histories and Texts: Refiguring the Diary of Samuel Pepys', *The Historical Journal*, 43:2: 407–31.

Dekker, Rudolf. 1995. 'Dutch Travel Journals from the Sixteenth to the Early Nineteenth Centuries', *Lias*, 22: 2: 277–99.

Din-Kariuki, Natalya. 2020. '"Strange Accidents": Navigating Conflict in Sir Thomas Smithes Voiage and Entertainment in Rushia (1605)', in *Travel and Conflict in the Early Modern World*, ed. Gábor Gelléri and Rachel Willie. New York: Routledge, 58–78.

Din-Kariuki, Natalya. 2023. 'Reading the Ottoman Empire: Intertextuality and Experience in Henry Blount's *Voyage into the Levant* (1636)', *The Review of English Studies*, 74:313: 47–63.

Dragstra, Henk, and Sheila Ottway, and Helen Wilcox (eds.). 2000. *Betraying Our Selves: Forms of Self-Representation in Early Modern English Texts.* Basingstoke: Macmillan.

Dugan, Holly. 2011. *The Ephemeral History of Perfume: Scent and Sense in Early Modern England.* Baltimore: Johns Hopkins University Press.

Dym, Jordana and Carla Lois. 2021. 'Bound Images: Maps, Books, and Reading in Material and Digital Contexts', *Word & Image*, 37:2, 119–41.

Earle, Rebecca. 2014. *The Body of the Conquistador*. Cambridge: Cambridge University Press.

Edge, Joanne. 2023. 'Taking it to Heart: Grief and Illness in Alice Thornton's Books'. *Alice Thornton's Books*. Accessed 25 May 2023. https://thornton.kdl.kcl.ac.uk/posts/blog/2022-12-19-grief-and-illness-thornton/.

Enenkel, Karl A. E. and Jan L. de Jong (eds.). 2019. *Artes Apodemicae and Early Modern Travel Culture, 1550–1700*. Leiden: Brill.

Farr, James R. and Guido Ruggiero (eds.). 2019. *Historicizing Life-Writing and Egodocuments in Early Modern Europe*. New York: Palgrave Macmillan.

Featherstone, Kerry. 2019. '"Picnics with the Mujaheddin": Paratexts and Personal Motivation in Travel Writing about Afghanistan', *Journeys: International Journal of Travel and Travel Writing*, 20:2: 1–19.

Forsdick, Charles (ed.). 2019. *Keywords for Travel Writing Studies: A Critical Glossary*. London: Anthem Press.

Frank, Arthur W. 1995. *The Wounded Storyteller: Body, Illness and Ethics*. Chicago: University of Chicago Press.

Fulbrook, Mary and Ulinka Rublack. 2010. 'In Relation: The "Social Self" and Ego-Documents', *German History*, 28:3: 263–72.

Fuller, Mary C. 2008. *Remembering the Early Modern Voyage: English Narratives in the Age of European Expansion*. New York: Palgrave.

Gallagher, John. 'The Italian London of John North: Cultural Contact and Linguistic Encounter in Early Modern England', *Renaissance Quarterly*, 70: 1 (March 1, 2017): 88–131.

Gentilcore, David. 2016. *Food and Health in Early Modern Europe: Diet, Medicine and Society, 1450-1800*. London: Bloomsbury.

Ghobrial, John-Paul A. 2014. 'The Secret Life of Elias of Babylon and the Uses of Global Microhistory', *Past & Present*, 222:1: 51–93.

Goldgar, Anne. 2020. 'Marketing Arctic Knowledge: Observation, Publication, and Affect in the 1630s', in Inger Leemans and Anne Goldgar (eds.) London: Routledge, pp. 204–227*Early Modern Knowledge Societies as Affective Economies*. Routledge, Taylor & Francis Group, 25.

Greenblatt, Stephen. 1984. *Renaissance Self-Fashioning: From More to Shakespeare*. Chicago: The University of Chicago Press

Hacke, Daniela, and Claudia Jarzebowski, and Hannes Ziegler (eds.). 2021. *Matters of Engagement: Emotions, Identity, and Cultural Contact in the Premodern World*. New York: Routledge.

Hadfield, Andrew. 1998. *Literature, Travel, and Colonial Writing in the English Renaissance, 1545–1625*. Oxford: Oxford University Press.

2009. 'Introduction: Does Shakespeare's Life Matter?' *Textual Practice*, 23:2: 181–99.

2017. *Lying in Early Modern English Culture: From the Oath of Supremacy to the Oath of Allegiance*. Oxford: Oxford University Press.

Hailwood, Mark and Brodie Waddell. 2023. 'Work and Identity in Early Modern England', *Transactions of the Royal Historical Society*, 1: December 2023, pp. 145–158.

Haydon, Liam. 2017. *An Analysis of Stephen Greenblatt's Renaissance Self-Fashioning: From More to Shakespeare*, Macat Library. London: Macat International.

Hodgkin, Katharine and Susannah Radstone (eds.). 2003. *Regimes of Memory*, 1st ed. London: Routledge.

Hodgkin, Katharine. 2016. 'Childhood and Loss in Early Modern Life Writing', *Parergon*, 33:2: 115–34. https://doi.org/10.1353/pgn.2016.0078.

2017. 'Autobiographical Writings', in *The Oxford Handbook of Early Modern English Literature and Religion*, eds. Andrew Hiscock and Helen Wilcox. Oxford: Oxford University Press, 207–22.

2020. 'Time and Space: Autobiographical Memory', in *A Cultural History of Memory in the Early Modern Age*, eds. Marek Tamm and Alessandro Arcangeli, *A Cultural History of Memory General Editors: Stefan Berger and Jeffrey Olick*. London, 37–55.

Holmberg, Eva Johanna. 2017. 'Writing the Travelling Self: Travel and Life-Writing in Peter Mundy's (1597–1667) Itinerarium Mundii', *Renaissance Studies*, 31:4: 608–25.

2019. 'Introduction: Renaissance and Early Modern Travel – Practice and Experience, 1500-1700: Introduction: Renaissance and Early Modern Travel', *Renaissance Studies*, 33:4: 515–23.

2021a. 'Fynes Moryson's Grief: Writing the Mobile Ailing Body in Seventeenth-Century England', *Cultural and Social History*, 18:1: 45–60.

2021b. '"Passages Recollected by Memory": Remembering the Levant Company in Seventeenth-Century Merchants' Life Writing', in *Trading Companies and Travel Knowledge in the Early Modern World*, eds. A. Laursen Brock, G. van Meersbergen and E. Smith. Abingdon: Routledge, Hakluyt Society Studies in the History of Travel; Vol.), 211–39.

2021c. 'Avoiding Conflict in the Early Modern Levant: Henry Blount's Adaptations in Ottoman lands', in *Travel and Conflict in the Early Modern World*, eds. Gábor Gelléri and Rachel Willie. New York: Routledge, 127–44.

2022. 'John Sanderson's Horrible Housemates'. *BL Untold Lives Blog*. https://blogs.bl.uk/untoldlives/2022/02/john-sandersons-horrible-house mates.html9.

Forthcoming 2024. 'An Unmoored Life: Mobility, Reading, and Life-Writing in Richard Norwood's (1590–1675) Confessions', Forthcoming in Huntington Library Quarterly.

Horden, Peregrine. 2005. 'Travel Sickness: Medicine and Mobility in the Mediterranean from Antiquity to the Renaissance', in *Rethinking the Mediterranean*, ed. William Vernon Harris. Oxford: Oxford University Press, 179–99.

Hubbard, Eleanor. 2021. *Englishmen at Sea: Labor and the Nation at the Dawn of Empire, 1570–1630*. New Haven: Yale University Press.

Hunt, Katherine. 2018. 'The Art of Changes: Bell-Ringing, Anagrams, and the Culture of Combination in Seventeenth- Century England', *Journal of Medieval and Early Modern Studies*, 48:2: 387–412.

Ivanič, Susanna. 2015. 'The Construction of Identity through Visual Intertextuality in a Bohemian Early Modern Travelogue', *Visual Communication*, 14:1: 49–72.

Jarvis, Robin. 2018. 'What Am I Still Doing Here?: Travel, Travel Writing, and Old Age', *Journeys*, 19:1: 88–106.

Jenner, Mark S. R. 2011. 'Follow Your Nose? Smell, Smelling, and Their Histories', *The American Historical Review*, 116:2: 335–51.

Kamps, Ivo and Jyotsna Singh (eds.). 2001. *Travel Knowledge: European 'Discoveries' in the Early Modern Period*. Basingstoke: Palgrave Macmillan.

Kew, Graham David. 1995. 'Shakespeare's Europe Revisited: The Unpublished "Itinerary" of Fynes Moryson (1566 – 1630)'. PhD, Birmingham, University of Birmingham.

Kinsley, Zoë. 2014. 'Narrating Travel, Narrating the Self: Considering Women's Travel Writing as Life Writing', *Bulletin of the John Rylands Library*, 90:2: 67–84.

Kinsley, Zoë. 2019. 'Travelogues, Diaries, Letters', in Nandini Das and Tim Youngs (eds.) *The Cambridge History of Travel Writing*. Cambridge: Cambridge University Press, 408–22.

Kuehn, Julia and Paul Smethurst (eds.). 2015. *New Directions in Travel Writing Studies*. New York: Palgrave Macmillan.

Kupperman, Karen Ordahl. 1984. 'Fear of Hot Climates in the Anglo-American Colonial Experience', *The William and Mary Quarterly*, 41:2: 213–40.

Kynan-Wilson, William. 2017. '"Painted by the Turcks Themselves": Reading Peter Mundy's Ottoman Costume Album in Context', in *The Mercantile Effect: Art and Exchange in the Islamicate World during the 17th and 18th Centuries*, eds. Sussan Babaie and Melanie Gibson. London: Gingko Library, 38–50.

Legassie, Shayne Aaron. 2017. *The Medieval Invention of Travel*. Chicago: Chicago University Press.

Leong, Elaine. 2013. 'Collecting Knowledge for the Family: Recipes, Gender and Practical Knowledge in the Early Modern English Household', *Centaurus; International Magazine of the History of Science and Medicine*, 55:2: 81–103.

Levy, Fred Jacob. 1974. 'Henry Peacham and the Art of Drawing', *Journal of the Warburg and Courtauld Institutes*, 37: 174–90.

Linte, Guillaume. 2022. '"Hot Climates" and Disease: Early Modern European Views of Tropical Environments', in *Disease and the Environment in the Medieval and Early Modern Worlds*, ed. Lori Jones, 1st ed. London: Routledge, 107–23.

Lynch, Kathleen. 2012. *Protestant Autobiography in the Seventeenth-Century Anglophone World*. Oxford: Oxford University Press.

MacLean, Gerald M. 2004a. 'Strolling in Syria with William Biddulph', *Criticism*, 46:3: 415–39.

   2004b. *The Rise of Oriental Travel: English Visitors to the Ottoman Empire, 1580–1720*. New York: Palgrave Macmillan.

Maczak, Antoni. 1995. *Travel in Early Modern Europe*. London: Polity.

Mansell, Charmian. 2021. 'Beyond the Home: Experiences of Female Service in Early Modern England', *Gender and History*, 33:1 (2021): 24–49

Marschke, Benjamin. 2022. 'Writing About the "Other" in One's Life: Life-Writing and Egodocuments of King Frederick William I of Prussia (1713–1740) as Historical Problem', in *Historicizing Life-Writing and Egodocuments in Early Modern Europe*, eds. James R. Farr and Guido Ruggiero. Cham: Springer International, 153–85.

Martin, John Jeffries. 2018. *Myths of Renaissance Individualism*. Basingstoke: Palgrave Macmillan.

Mather, James. 2009. *Pashas: Traders and Travellers in the Islamic World*. New Haven: Yale University Press.

Mayer, Thomas Frederick and Daniel Robert Woolf (eds.). 1995. *The Rhetorics of Life-Writing in Early Modern Europe: Forms of Biography from Cassandra Fedele to Louis XIV*. Ann Arbor: University of Michigan Press.

Midura, Rachel. 2021. 'Itinerating Europe: Early Modern Spatial Networks in Printed Itineraries, 1545–1700', *Journal of Social History*, 54:4: 1023–63, shab011, https://doi.org/10.1093/jsh/shab011.

Mitchell, Silvia Z. 2022. 'Everard Nithard's *Memorias*: The Jesuit Confessor's Quest for Re-fashioning the Self, People, and Events', in *Historicizing Life-Writing and Egodocuments in Early Modern Europe*, eds. James R. Farr and Guido Ruggiero. Cham: Palgrave Macmillan, 107–35.

Mitsi, Efterpi. 2017. *Greece in Early English Travel Writing, 1596–1682*. Cham: Palgrave Macmillan, 31–32.

Mol, Annemarie. 2021. *Eating in Theory*. Durham: Duke University Press.

Mousley, Andy. 2009. 'Early Modern Autobiography, History and Human Testimony: The Autobiography of Thomas Whythorne', *Textual Practice*, 23:2: 267–87.

Mundy, Peter. 1907. *The Travels of Peter Mundy in Europe and Asia 1608-1667 / Peter Mundy. Vol 1, Travels in Europe 1608–1628*, eds. Richard Carnac Temple. Cambridge: Hakluyt Society.

    1914. *The Travels of Peter Mundy in Europe and Asia, 1608–1667*, eds. Richard Carnac Temple. *Vol. II. Travels in Asia, 1628–1634*. London: Printed for the Hakluyt Society.

    2010. *Travels of Peter Mundy, in Europe and Asia, 1608-1667: Volume IV: Travels in Europe 1639-1647*. Farnham, Surrey, GBR: Hakluyt Society, 97–8.

Murphy, Emilie. 2021. University of York: 'Earwitnesses: Early Modern Anglophone Travellers and the Dissemination of Religious Knowledge'. Presented at the RSA Virtual.

Netzloff, Mark. 2020. *Agents beyond the State: The Writings of English Travelers, Soldiers, and Diplomats in Early Modern Europe*. Oxford: Oxford University Press.

Newton, Hannah. 2011. '"Very Sore Nights and Days": The Child's Experience of Illness in Early Modern England, c.1580–1720', *Medical History*, 55:2: 153–82.

    2015. '"Nature Concocts and Expels": The Agents and Processes of Recovery from Disease in Early Modern England', *Social History of Medicine*, 28:3: 465–86.

    2018. *Misery to Mirth: Recovery from Illness in Early Modern England*. Oxford: Oxford University Press.

Nunn, Hillary M. 2020. 'Local Waters and Notions of Home in Early Modern Recipe Manuscripts', *Journal for Early Modern Cultural Studies*, 20:1: 59–82.

O'Donnell, Paris. 2009. 'Pilgrimage or "Anti-Pilgrimage"? Uses of Mementoes and Relics in English and Scottish Narratives of Travel to Jerusalem, 1596–1632'. *Studies in Travel Writing*, 13:2: 125–39. https://doi.org/10.1080/13645140902857232.

OED Online. 2022. Oxford University Press. www-oed-com.libproxy.helsinki.fi/view/Entry/143117?rskey=70nspU&result=1&isAdvanced=false. Accessed 2 February 2023.

Ord, Melanie. 2008. *Travel and Experience in Early Modern English Literature*. Basingstoke: Macmillan.

Palmer, Philip S. 2011. '"By My Owne Experience or the Most Probablest Relation off Others": Manuscript Travel Writing and Peter Mundy's "Relation" of Constantinople (1617-20),' in *Early Modern England and Islamic Worlds*, eds. Bernadette Andrea and Linda McJannet. New York: Palgrave Macmillan, 123–138.

Pannell, Lindsay B. 2017. 'Viperous Breathings: The Miasma Theory in Early Modern England'. https://doi.org/10/103.

Parkinson, Tom. 2012. 'Finding Fynes: Moryson's Biography and the Latin Manuscript of Part One of the Itenerary (1617).' Thesis, Queen Mary University of London. http://qmro.qmul.ac.uk/xmlui/handle/123456789/8696.

Parr, Anthony. 2012. '"Going to Constantinople": English Wager-Journeys to the Ottoman World in the Early-Modern Period', *Studies in Travel Writing*, 16:4: 349–61.

Paul, K. Tawny. 2018. 'Accounting for Men's Work: Multiple Employments and Occupational Identities in Early Modern England', *History Workshop Journal*, 85: 26–46.

Pettinger, Alasdair and Tim Youngs (eds.). 2020. *The Routledge Research Companion to Travel Writing*. London: Routledge.

Pfannebecker, Mareile. 2017. ' "Lying by Authority": Travel Dissimulations in Fynes Moryson's *Itinerary.*' *Renaissance Studies*, 31:4: 569–85.

Pollmann, Judith. 2017. *Memory in Early Modern Europe, 1500–1800*. Oxford: Oxford University Press.

Pritchard, Alan. 2005. *English Biography in the Seventeenth Century: A Critical Survey*. Toronto: University of Toronto Press.

Radway, Robyn Dora. 2023. *Portraits of Empires: Habsburg Albums from the German House in Ottoman Constantinople.*Bloomington: Indiana University Press.

Raiswell, Richard. 2004. 'Mundy, Peter (b. c. 1596, d. in or after 1667), Traveller and Diarist'. *Oxford Dictionary of National Biography.* Accessed 1 June 2023. www.oxforddnb.com/view/10.1093/ref:odnb/9780198614128.001.0001/odnb-9780198614128-e-19540.

Rankin, Alisha. 2016. *Secrets and Knowledge in Medicine and Science, 1500–1800*. London: Routledge.

Raunio, Anu. 2019. 'Crossing Borders in the Age of Confessionalization: Seventeenth-Century Italian Travel Writing on the North', *Renaissance Studies*, 33: 624–38.

Reinburg, Virginia. 2016. 'Archives, Eyewitnesses and Rumours: Writing about Shrines in Early Modern France', *Past & Present*, 230:suppl. 11: 171–90.

Renders, Hans, and Binne de Haan, and Jonne Harsma (eds.). 2017. *The Biographical Turn: Lives in History.* London: Routledge.

Roberts, Rosie. 2012. *Ongoing Mobility Trajectories: Lived Experiences of Global Migration.* Singapore: Springer.

Rolfe, Kirsty. 2020. 'Fatal and Memorable: Plague, Providence and War in English Texts, 1625-6', *The Seventeenth Century*, 35:3: 293–314.

Rosenwein, Barbara H. 2002. 'Worrying about Emotions in History', *The American Historical Review*, 107:3: 821–45.

Rothman, E. Natalie. 2012. *Brokering Empire: Trans-Imperial Subjects between Venice and Istanbul.* Ithaca: Cornell University Press.

Rubiés, Joan-Pau. 2000a. 'Travel Writing as a Genre: Facts, Fictions and the Invention of a Scientific Discourse in Early Modern Europe.' *Journeys*, 1:1:5–35.

2000b. *Travel and Ethnology in the Renaissance. South India through European Eyes, 1250–1625.* Cambridge: Cambridge University Press.

2017. 'Were Early Modern Europeans Racist?', in *Ideas of 'Race' in the History of the Humanities*, eds. Amos. Morris-Reich and Dirk Rupnow. Palgrave Critical Studies of Antisemitism and Racism. Cham: Palgrave Macmillan, 33–87.

Salzberg, Rosa. 2023. *The Renaissance on the Road: Mobility, Migration and Cultural Exchange.* Elements in the Renaissance. Cambridge: Cambridge University Press.

Samson, Alexander. 2009. 'The Colour of the Country': English Travellers in Spain, 1604–1625. *Studies in Travel Writing*, 13:111–24.

Sau, Pablo Hernández and Francisco A. Eissa-Barroso. 2022. 'Introduction: "Ongoing" Mobilities in the Early-Modern Spanish World', *Journal of Iberian and Latin American Studies*, 28:3: 329–43.

Schmidt, Benjamin. 2015. *Inventing Exoticism: Geography, Globalism, and Europe's Early Modern World.* Philadelphia: University of Pennsylvania Press.

Scott-Warren, Jason. 2016. 'Early Modern Bookkeeping and Life-Writing Revisited: Accounting for Richard Stonley', *Past & Present*, 230:suppl. 11: 151–70.

Sell, Jonathan P. A. 2012. 'Embodying Truth in Early Modern English Travel Writing', *Studies in Travel Writing*, 16:3: 227–41.

Shapin, Steven. 1994. *Social History of Truth. Civility and Science in Seventeenth-Century England.* Chicago: University of Chicago Press.

Sharpe, Kevin and Steven N. Zwicker (eds.). 2008. *Writing Lives: Biography and Textuality, Identity and Representation in Early Modern England.* Oxford: Oxford University Press.

Shepard, Alexandra. 2015. *Accounting for Oneself: Worth, Status, & the Social Order in Early Modern England*. : Oxford: Oxford University Press.

Sherman, William H. 2010. *Used Books: Marking Readers in Renaissance England*. Philadelphia: University of Pennsylvania Press.

Silver, Sean. 2015. 'John Evelyn and Numismata: Material History and Autobiography', *Word & Image*, 31:3: 331–42.

Singh, Jyotsna G. (ed.). 2009. *A Companion to the Global Renaissance*: *English Literature and Culture in the Era of Expansion*, 1st ed. Chichester:Wiley-Blackwell.

Skura, Meredith Anne. 2008. *Tudor Autobiography: Listening for Inwardness*. Chicago: University of Chicago Press.

Smith, Mark M. 2015. *The Smell of Battle, the Taste of Siege: A Sensory History of the Civil War*. New York: Oxford University Press.

Smith, Pamela and Paula Findlen (eds.). 2013. *Merchants and Marvels: Commerce Science and Art in Early Modern Europe: Commerce, Science, and Art in Early Modern Europe*. New York: Routledge.

Smith, Pamela H. 2018. *The Body of the Artisan: Art and Experience in the Scientific Revolution*. Chicago: University of Chicago Press.

Smyth, Adam. 2010. *Autobiography in Early Modern England*. Cambridge: Cambridge University Press.

2018. *Material Texts in Early Modern England*. Cambridge: Cambridge University Press.

Stewart, Alan. 2008. *Shakespeare's Letters*. Oxford: Oxford University Press.

Stewart, Alan. 2018. *The Oxford History of Life Writing: Volume 2. Early Modern*. Oxford History of Life-Writing. Oxford: Oxford University Press.

Stolberg, Michael. 2011. *Experiencing Illness and the Sick Body in Early Modern Europe*. Basingstoke: Palgrave Macmillan.

Stoye, John. 1989. *English Travellers Abroad, 1604-1667: Their Influence on English Society and Politics* (1952), Revised ed. New Haven:Yale University Press.

Summerfield, Penny. 2019. *Histories of the Self: Personal Narratives and Historical Practice*. London: Routledge.

Swann, Elizabeth L. 2018. *Taste and Knowledge in Early Modern England*. Cambridge: Cambridge University Press.

Sweet, Rosemary, and Gerrit Verhoeven, and Sarah Goldsmith (eds.). 2017. *Beyond the Grand Tour: Northern Metropolises and Early Modern Travel Behaviour*. New York: Routledge.

Tarantino, Giovanni and Charles Zika (eds.). 2019. *Feeling Exclusion: Religious Conflict, Exile and Emotions in Early Modern Europe*. London: Routledge.

Thompson, Carl. 2007. *The Suffering Traveller and the Romantic Imagination.* Oxford: Oxford University Press.

Thorley, David. 2016. *Writing Illness and Identity in Seventeenth-Century Britain.* London: Palgrave Macmillan.

Tullett, William. 2023. *Smell and the Past: Noses, Archives, Narratives.* New York: Bloomsbury Academic.

Waddell, Brodie. 2019. '"Verses of My Owne Making": Literacy, Work, and Social Identity in Early Modern England', *Journal of Social History*, 54:1 (Fall 2020), 161–184.

Walsham, Alexandra. 2023. *Generations: Age, Ancestry and Memory in the English Reformations.* Oxford: Oxford University Press.

Whitehead, Maurice. 2016. *English Jesuit Education: Expulsion, Suppression, Survival and Restoration*, 1762–1803, London and New York: Routledge, p. 116.

Williams, Mark R. F. 2019. 'The Inner Lives of Early Modern Travel', *The Historical Journal*, 62:2: 349–73

2022. 'Experiencing Time in the Early English East India Company', *The Historical Journal*, 65 :5 (December 2022) 1175–96.

Williamson, Elizabeth. 2016. '"Fishing after News" and the Ars Apodemica: The Intelligencing Role of the Educational Traveller in the Late Sixteenth Century', in Joad Raymond and Noah Moxham (eds.) *News Networks in Early Modern Europe.* Leiden: Brill, 542–62.

Winchcombe, Rachel. 2022. 'Foodways and Emotional Communities in Early Colonial Virginia', *Environment and History*, 28:3: 397–414.

Wood, Alfred Cecil. 1964. *A History of the Levant Company.* London: Frank Cass.

Wood, Andy. 2013. *The Memory of the People: Custom and Popular Senses of the Past in Early Modern England.* Cambridge: Cambridge University Press.

Wyatt, Anna. 2021. '"On the Eminent Dr Edward Brown's Travels": A Familial Network of Creation in the Philosophical Transactions.' *Studies in Philology*, 118:2: 368–98.

Youngs, Tim. 2019. 'Hearing', in Alasdair Pettinger and Tim Youngs (eds.) *The Routledge Research Companion to Travel Writing.* London: Routledge, 208–21.

Zenobi, Luca. 2021. 'Mobility and Urban Space in Early Modern Europe: An Introduction', *Journal of Early Modern History*, 25:1–2: 1–10.

Cambridge Elements ≡

Travel Writing

Nandini Das

University of Oxford

Nandini Das is a literary scholar and cultural historian, Professor of Early Modern Literature and Culture at the University of Oxford, and Fellow of Exeter College, Oxford. With Tim Youngs, she has co-edited The Cambridge History of Travel Writing (2019), and published widely on early modern English literature, cross-cultural encounters, and travel accounts.

Tim Youngs

Nottingham Trent University

Tim Youngs is Professor of English and Travel Studies at Nottingham Trent University. His books include The Cambridge Companion to Travel Writing (edited with Peter Hulme, 2002), The Cambridge Introduction to Travel Writing (2013), and The Cambridge History of Travel Writing (edited with Nandini Das, 2019). He edits the journal Studies in Travel Writing.

About the Series

Travel writing is enormously varied. It consists of several different forms and has a long history across many cultures. This series aims to reflect that diversity, offering exciting studies of a range of travel texts and topics. The Elements further advance the latest thinking in travel writing, extending previous work and opening up the field to fresh readings and subjects of inquiry.

Cambridge Elements ☰

Travel Writing

Elements in the Series